Don't Drive on the Sidewalk!

(Inspirations through the DETOURS of Life!)

By

Gail M. Renderman

PRESS

May God always
guide your roads
and brighten your
life!!

Blessings
Gail Renderman

That I may publish with the voice of thanksgiving, and tell of all thy wondrous works.

Psalm 26:7

Dear Heavenly Father

I do not know how long my journey is,
Or where my roads may lead,
I only ask that you take my hand,
And let me bring a smile to others before I leave.

Dedication

To Richard, Joseph and Jennifer
My reasons to love, laugh at life and
my strength to soar to great heights.
You are the wind beneath my wings!

Contents

❧∞❧

Acknowledgments

With great appreciation to:

Our heavenly father who has been my guide all of my life. I give glory to His wondrous works. He is my Salvation and has renewed my heart, and spirit, to SOAR as with Eagles Wings. "I CAN DO all things because He strengthens me!" Philippians 4:13

My husband, Richard, and children, Joseph and Jennifer, who are the lights of my life. You have given me your unconditional love, support and encouragement to handle all of my illnesses, surgeries and living with Myasthenia Gravis. You are the wind beneath my wings. My love for you goes beyond the stars. I thank you for helping me laugh through the journey of life.

My parents, Marge and Del Thill, my sisters, mother-in-law, Thelma Renderman and extended family members for your belief in my ability to write this and for helping me rise above the storms.

My friends for your encouragement and always being by my side. You have lifted me up, warmed my heart and filled me with laughter.

My customers, sister consultants and directors in my world of Mary Kay Cosmetics, for your enthusiasm and positive encouragement. You have inspired me to "Dream Big" and reach for the Stars, even when I can't walk.

Drs. Robert H. and Robert A. Schuller, of the Crystal Cathedral

Ministries. Your positive "Hour of Power" messages that helped me conquer many mountains.

Renée Bondi and your music ministry, for renewing my soul. Your faith and courage have shown me that we all have the "Ability" to rise above adversity.

The Myasthenia Gravis Support Groups for your efforts in helping other MG patients and for spreading "Snowflake" cheer around the world.

Last, but not least, my grandmother, the late Della Mitchell, and my father-in-law, the late Melvin Renderman, for teaching me the most important lessons in life: We must have determination, courage, kindness, a strong belief and the dignity to go on through any pain that life presents.

Introduction

"They that wait upon the Lord shall renew their strength; they shall mount up as with wings of eagles; they shall run, and not be weary; and they shall walk, and not faint."

Isaiah 40:31

Years ago, I chose Isaiah 40:31 as my motto in life, because *WAITING* was *NOT* one of my strong suits. I was a Mover and a Doer! Constantly on the go! I loved to work from sunrise to sunset and thought that nothing could stop me from my goals. Then I was faced with family struggles, illnesses, surgeries and a life changing disorder. I soon realized that detours are going to happen, whether we want them to or not. It's important to *NEVER QUIT!*

How determined are you? If you were on a cross country trip, and half way there you came upon a road closed sign, would you turn around and forget about the rest of your journey? Or would you look for a new road to help you reach your destination? Detours are not only for those who drive, but also for everyone who is trying to get through the journey of life. Rough Roads, Dead End, One Way, Road Closed, Bridge Out, Be Prepared To Stop, Lane Closed and Do Not Enter signs seem to be everywhere. We all have them: job losses, loneliness, family changes, marital issues, money problems, accidents, illnesses and even death.

I know how challenges can affect us, our moods, our families and our will to go on! I believe that God places tough times before us, to build us for greater things to come. Laughter, a positive attitude and a strong faith can make it easier to get through the twist, turns, bumps and potholes on the roughest roads.

Have you ever driven on a detour by yourself? It can be pretty scary! But the sights might be even more SPECTACULAR than on your original path! We may be traveling by ourselves, but we're never alone when we ask God to ride with us. Remember that He's got the best view of the road. He can see what's ahead and can help us through the obstacles, just watch out when God decides to drive!

You may not see it at this moment, but in time you will grow from each experience. You will know that God has rebuilt your strength and courage. When you soar, as with eagle's wings, you'll know that God has lifted you up and carried you higher than you ever thought you could go. *NEVER GIVE IN,* always go on with *JOY* in your heart!

Sit back, buckle up and we'll have some fun traveling through the detours of life together, without driving on the sidewalk!

CHAPTER 1

Driven By A Dream

"I say unto you, If ye have faith as a grain of mustard seed, ye shall say unto this mountain, Remove hence to yonder place; and it shall remove and nothing shall be impossible unto you."

Matthew 17:20

The Grandest Rose

*(This is dedicated in memory of two special women: My
grandmother, Della Mitchell, who taught me to have courage and
kindness through the pain; and Mary Kay Ash, Founder of Mary
Kay Cosmetics, who taught people around the world, in order to
WIN in life, you must HELP others, have FAITH and NEVER
QUIT! Their love will forever blossom!)*

If a person could be a flower,
She was the Grandest Rose!
Strong, yet gentle and sweet,
From her head down to her toes.

Her arms were always out,
Like leaves stretched in the air,
Opened to give warm hugs,
To show how much she cared.

She had great strength and courage,
Like the stem that holds the rose.
She was one determined lady,
As everybody knows.

And, yes, just like the thorns,
She had her aches and pains,
But she always had a smile,
Her kindness was our gain.

Finally, like the blossom,
She was so soft and sweet.
It made her one of the most loved ladies,
By everyone she'd meet.

Yes, if a person could be a flower,
The love for life she showed,
Made her dear to all our hearts,
God gave us *THE GRANDEST ROSE!*

"The voice of him that crieth in the wilderness, Prepare ye the way of the Lord, make straight in the desert a highway for our God. Every valley shall be exalted, and every mountain and hill shall be made low: and the crooked shall be made straight, and the rough places plain:"

Isaiah 40:3-4

When God Decides To Drive

When God decides to drive, don't tell Him ...."NO!"
Put your seat belt on and go with His flow.

Hang onto your hat and get ready to laugh,
He'll drive through the obstacles out in His path.

He's got a mighty plan and in His mighty way,
Your world will be upturned, so hang on today.

There will be rocks and branches, twists and turns,
Your emotions will be jolted; your stomach will churn.

Open your heart and open your mind,
God has picked you out; He'll be by your side.

But, I wanted to drive in just my own way,
When I tried to switch places it all went astray.

My courage was down; my self-esteem was low,
I was so confused; I didn't know where to go.

I decided to give in, put the wheel in God's hand,
Asked Him to guide me and show me His plans.

He had a smile on His face and a sparkle in His eyes,
He said "Buckle up and get ready to fly!"

So, when God decides to drive, don't tell Him ... "NO!"
Hand over the keys and give Him the control!

"The things which are impossible with men are possible with God."

Luke 18:27

All Things Are Possible

I start to climb my ladder and, when I slip, I feel a guiding hand,
That helps me reach the dreams I seek and lets me know I can.

The dreams of great and wonderful things that I know I can achieve,
Showing me all things are possible, if only I Believe.

So, I thank the Lord every day, for always guiding me through,
For the wonderful friends in my life, especially for "YOU"!

Your encouragement and patience, time and time again,
Shows through in all that you do, you're such a Special Friend.

As a Christian you live your faith for the entire world to see.
You stand tough, when times are rough, and you're always there for me.

May the Lord cast His blessings and give you strength each day,
To help you reach the goals you set and guide you along the way.

Your leadership and love are inspiring, that's so true.
You've taught me that all things are possible and I thank the Lord for you.

"They that wait upon the Lord shall renew their strength; they shall mount up with wings as eagles; they shall run, and not be weary; and they shall walk, and not faint."

Isaiah 40:31

Where The Eagles Dare To Soar

An eagle, a sign of strength, wings spread out wide,
Just watch its graceful body, as it soars up in the sky.

I marvel at its beauty, head held high and proud,
Its eyes fixed on the target, as it swoops toward the ground.

They don't travel in flocks like geese, they fly out on their own.
The elements don't stop them, they dare to soar alone.

They endure the stormiest of weather, fly right through it all.
Soaring to the greatest heights, they rise to the call.

When I think of the animal, I most resemble in my life,
The eagle is the one, because it soars through all its strife.

The eagle can fly in places, that others birds dare not go.
It soars on through all the seasons, summer rains and winter snow.

I'm proud to say I'm an eagle! I let nothing stop me in my tracks.
And like an eagle I'm strong enough, to let adversity run off my back.

I shall take on new challenges, each and every day.
I'll become a stronger eagle, with the courage to make it all the way.

When obstacles and sicknesses, try to take me down,
I won't become discouraged, while I rest upon the ground.

I will not give in today, for a goal I have in sight.
It's planted firmly in my head, until I again can take my flight.

When my life is finished, and I reach God's golden door,
I can say "I've done my best,
I went — Where The Eagles Dare To Soar!"

"Give thanks unto the Lord, call upon his name, make known his deeds among the people. Sing unto him, sing psalms unto him, talk ye of all his wondrous works. Glory ye in his holy name: let the heart of them rejoice that seek the Lord. Seek the Lord and his strength, seek his face continually. Remember his marvellous works that he hath done, his wonders, and the judgments of his mouth;"

1 Chronicles 16:8-12

Be Thankful

BE THANKFUL - for the wonderful people that touch your life in special ways.

BE THANKFUL - for challenges, they are the stepping stones to STRENGTH.

BE THANKFUL - for the determination to go on, even when you don't feel like it.

BE THANKFUL - for learning to take a negative situation and turn it into positive results.

BE THANKFUL - that a stranger one day, can become a friend for life.

BE THANKFUL - for your family. Say loving things to them each day, you never know if you'll have tomorrow to do the same.

BE THANKFUL - for the ability to keep going, long after you want to call it quits.

BE THANKFUL - for the people who aren't perfect. They teach us that winning doesn't come from perfection, but rather from optimism and a positive attitude.

BE THANKFUL - that you and your friends can all be different, yet support each other with your strengths.

BE THANKFUL - for children, they teach us to laugh and enjoy the simple things in life.

BE THANKFUL - for learning that maturity doesn't mean growing older, but growing wiser.

BE THANKFUL - that love doesn't need a degree, but a caring heart to help others.

BE THANKFUL - for understanding people. They teach us that it takes time to become the person that we want to be.

BE THANKFUL - for the obstacles that teach you perseverance.

BE THANKFUL - for learning that success doesn't come overnight, but it is built over time.

BE THANKFUL - for the fortitude to fight off defeat.

BE THANKFUL - that money isn't everything in life, but your attitude is.

BE THANKFUL - for finding out that heroes can be spouses, children, family members or good friends.

BE THANKFUL - for every day that you can get out of bed, because there may be a day when you can't.

BE THANKFUL - for learning that abundance is not what you have in life, but what you give to life.

BE THANKFUL - for realizing that you can't give up. You have to go on and *NEVER QUIT!*

BE THANKFUL - for knowing that with *GOD* you'll have every-thing you NEED in life!

"I call heaven and earth to record this day against you, that I have set before you life and death, blessing and cursing: therefore choose life, that both thou and thy seed may live:"

Deuteronomy 30:19.

"If Today"

IF TODAY .... Your days were numbered and you only had a few,
Would you make the most of every one, or waste them being blue?

Would you give a helping hand, to brighten someone's day?
Or flash a friendly smile, to all that passed your way?

Would you give a caring wave, to anyone you meet,
Say "Good Morning! It's nice to see you," to strangers on the street?

Would you treat your family members, as nice as you treat friends?
Would you take some tension out of life, and have more fun again?

Would you do something for others, each and every day,
Not grumble about the housework, or the driver in your way?

Would you say "I LOVE YOU" more, to those near your heart?
Well, you might not have tomorrow, so TODAY'S the time TO START!

IF TODAY....Was your last on Earth and
you did kind things with your time,
You wouldn't have to worry about tomorrow,
or regrets for days gone by!

So make the most of TODAY and the treasures you've been given.
Touch a life, pass on a smile, and your rewards will be in Heaven!

"But as for me, I will walk in mine integrity: redeem me, and be merciful unto me."

Psalm 26:11

A Diamond ... Shines Under Pressure

A diamond in the rough,
A simple piece of coal,
When tested under years of pressure,
Will shine above them all.

The diamond.... A gracious symbol,
Of elegance and class,
Has proven to be the most valuable gem,
And the strongest 'til the last.

A person, though made of flesh and bone,
Can be like a diamond in the rough,
When tested under adverse pressures,
Finds the strength to be so tough.

Though the coal inside that person,
Might be flaming mighty hot,
They gleam like a diamond on the outside,
To show the integrity they've got.

An aura of confidence,
Self discipline and strong will,
They ask God for help through the fight,
And they come out shining still.

So next time you are tested,
And your trials may be so rough,
Remember you have the strength of a diamond,
So SHINE ON, though your life may be tough.

"I can do all things through Christ which strengtheneth me."

Philippians 4:13

When Dreams Are Tossed And Blown!

When I was young, just out of my teens,
I had great visions. I had BIG DREAMS!
The world was mine, I would shoot for the stars,
I wanted it all, big house and big cars.

Then someone told me, "Your dreams aren't real."
"You have to tone them down!" My goals they did steal.
But I am a believer, so I thought "What the heck!"
"I will reach my goals, if I stick out my neck."

So on with believing, my plans fixed to go,
Then a sudden illness hit me, my dreams took a blow.
"Do I stop working now, give up today?"
It didn't make sense, so I created a way.

On with my march, on with my plans,
I was so determined, I took a new stand.
Over, under, or through, I would find a way.
I wouldn't give in, not now, not today!

Things were going good, my efforts building fine,
When my illness got worse, it confused my mind.
"What do I do? Which way can I turn?"
My thoughts up-dumped. My stomach did churn.

34

"Forget the dream? That's not my style!"
So I'll keep on trying, and fight for a while!
I gathered my strength, put a smile on my face,
I continued to work, with undying faith.

As the illness takes its toll, I do what I can.
I won't give up the goal, I'll make a new plan.
And when my dreams seem tossed and blown,
I know God will see me through, I'm never alone!

So if God's given you a dream, hold on to it tight.
Remember that nothing is WON, without courage and fight.
Your goals can be achieved, work hard and don't STOP,
"NEVER GIVING UP" on yourself, will take you to THE TOP!

Have determination each day to get out of bed,
Put a smile on your face and hold up your head.
For battles are WON, not by the swift or the fast,
But by the person who is UNDISCOURAGEABLE 'til the last!

"I am come that they might have life, and that they might have it more abundantly. I am the good shepherd: the good shepherd giveth his life for the sheep."

John 10:10-11

Abundant Living

Abundant Living… When you take the time to stop and look, you'll see it everywhere.

Abundant Living… Is not in how much you have, but in how much you give and share.

Abundant Living… It surrounds us like the wind, just watch an eagle soaring in flight.

Abundant Living… It's sitting and listening quietly, as you hear God's creatures playing at night.

Abundant Living… You'll see it in the trees and flowers that God planted on this earth.

Abundant Living… You'll see it in the joyful faces, just after a baby's birth.

Abundant Living… It's in the mountains, valleys and fields across this land.

Abundant Living… It's knowing that God will change the seasons and bring them back again.

Abundant Living… It isn't who has the most money or the biggest house upon the hill.

Abundant Living… It comes from letting God guide your life and following His will.

"Be strong and of a good courage, fear not, nor be afraid of them: for the Lord thy God, he it is that doth go with thee; he will not fail thee, nor forsake thee."

Deuteronomy 31:6

If You Fail ... So What!

If you fail ... So What! At least you can say that you've tried.
How can you reach the stars if you don't venture into the sky?

If you fail ... So What! At least you got up off your seat.
You can't succeed at something unless you're willing to face defeat.

If you fail ... So What! Will others make fun of you?
You won't become a stronger person until you're ready to be tested too.

If you fail ... So What! You'll be helping people along the way.
Your efforts will not be in vain when you can brighten someone's day.

If you fail ... So What! You have dreams and goals in mind.
If you don't work at them you'll just be wasting time.

If you fail ... So What! Success can not be won,
Unless there are mountains to be climbed and obstacles to overcome.

If you fail ... So What! God planted a dream deep inside,
You need to hand the controls to Him and get ready for Him to drive.

If you fail ... So What! Impossible dreams can come true!
I'm willing to give it a try, tell me ... Are You?

"I am come a light into the world, that whosoever believeth in me should not abide in darkness."

John 12:46

"One Star"

"One Star" ... that shines so bright,
On this dark and lonely night,
I have to hold on to belief,
That someone is watching over me.

"One Star" ... for courage, so I can reach my goal,
People think that I'm too old and my body's too slow,
But I'll hang tough and then they will see,
That my spirit and fight will set me free.

"One Star" ... as I look into the far off sky,
I wonder what the dreams are that others let by,
When I think of this huge goal it could bring me to tears,
But if I don't try I won't overcome my fears.

"One Star"... God gave me the ability and He has a plan,
I know His powers are great, so I'll take a stand,
I place my trust in Him, all fears set aside,
"One Star" ... My Lord, my eternal guide.

Always Believe In A Dream

God gives us Challenges and Detours,
Not as an excuse for us to fail,
But as a reason to BELIEVE in Miracles!
We never know where our roads will lead,
We must help others to find new paths in life,
We must travel on with Pride and Courage,
And we must ALWAYS BELIEVE IN A DREAM!

CHAPTER 2

Buckle Up ...
Car Seats And Careers

"Lo, children are an heritage of the Lord: and the fruit of the womb is his reward."

Psalm 127:3

Children — Our Gifts From God ...

Children are not ours to keep,
They are gifts from the One above.
They are given to us for a short time,
To hold and cuddle and love.

The day our gifts arrive,
We count their fingers and their toes,
We marvel at their tiny bodies,
Their pink cheeks and little nose.

God sends them to teach us lessons,
Which we all need to learn,
For what is important in life,
Is not how much we earn.

God has a plan all right,
He is very wise that way,
Before our gifts were delivered,
Work consumed our day.

But when we hold our little presents,
Time comes to a stop,
Our priorities seem to shift,
Now we are moms and pops.

Somehow all those meetings,
Being the best and winning the fight,
Do not seem as important,
As kissing our children good night.

And as our little gifts grow,
We hold them closer to our hearts,
For the lessons we learn from our children,
Will really make us smart!

"Many, O Lord my God, are thy wonderful works which thou hast done, and thy thoughts which are to us-ward: they cannot be reckoned up in order unto thee: if I would declare and speak of them, they are more than can be numbered."

Psalm 40:5

The Creation Of Mom

How God created *MOMS,*
We can only strive to guess,
Picturing Him at His workstation,
I'm sure He had quite a mess.

Her parts ... had to be flexible,
And yet be so soft,
She had to have nerves of steel,
To show little ones who was boss.

Her arms ... had to be gentle,
And still very strong,
To give warm hugs when needed,
And have strength to carry on.

Her eyes ... had to have compassion,
Yet rotate around inside,
To keep a watch on her children,
Especially when they had something to hide.

Her ears ... had to be good for listening,
And hearing between the lines,
For when a friend had a problem and needed to talk,
Or for getting the truth out from a lie.

Her shoulders ... had to be so soft,
But be able to carry the load,
For cuddling with her special other,
Or for lending when a world began to unfold.

Her hands ... needed to be nimble,
And yet be really quick,
For creating all those special touches,
Or taking care of her family when they are sick.

Her legs ... had to have super strength,
But fold as a lap,
For carrying her through 'til all hours of the night,
Or for when a child needed a nap.

Her mind ... had to be made,
Out of a material so tough,
To think things through, keep the schedules straight,
And still show kindness and love.

Her body ... had to be washable,
But yet needed a rosy glow,
To soak in a tub after a hard day's work,
Yet be endurable when she was on the go.

Yes, God had His work cut out,
And He had to get things just right,
He created the world in six days,
But creating *MOM* kept Him going many nights.

"How excellent is thy lovingkindness, O God! therefore the children of men put their trust under the shadow of thy wings."

Psalm 36:7

"Daddy!"

I remember walking by his side,
He seemed so strong and tall,
My daddy was my savior in life,
He'd pick me up when I would fall.

Every night when he'd come home,
I'd run quick as a snap,
I couldn't wait to see him again,
And cuddle on his lap.

He'd greet me with open arms,
And I realized something too,
His hugs felt even better,
When I was sad and blue.

Sometimes I'd get into trouble,
He'd tell me we needed to talk,
Instead of punishing me, he'd hold my hand,
And ask me questions while we walked.

It's the same way with our heavenly Father,
His arms are always open wide,
He's there when I need a little chat,
And when things go wrong, He's right by my side.

So when my own dad is no longer here,
I know I'll never have to fret,
For with the Lord close at hand,
My father's love I won't forget.

"And said unto them, Whosoever shall receive this child in my name receiveth me: and whosoever shall receive me receiveth him that sent me: for he that is least among you all, the same shall be great."

Luke 9:48

Lollipops And Rainbows

Children will delight in the simplest of things.
Watch their eyes light up when they see bright colors,
Like lollipops and rainbows.

They get all giggly when you help them make a tent from sheets,
And crawl inside to spend time at their level.
They'll hold on tight when you give them a hug.

They find new things everywhere they go.
They love to stop and pick flowers.
They will lay in the yard for hours on end
and look up at the cloud shapes.
The stars at night help them dream of wonderful places.

They love to go to the park to swing, run and simply be free.
They can bring a smile to the oldest of faces.
Even grandpas can't resist little ones crawling up on their laps.

They will make you stop what you
are doing to fly a kite on a windy day.
And, once out there, you'll remember
what is was like to have so much fun.
They'll find every puddle to jump in,
but don't be mad, you did the same thing.

They'll bring home lost puppies And try to hide them in their rooms,
But all the extra food leaving the kitchen will give them away.
They can make the worst of days
all right simply by yelling MOMMY or DADDY!

They'll cuddle up with their teddy bears at night,
hoping that you'll spend time and read them a story.
They'll find ways over or through All the toys that are on their floors.

And when they are sound asleep, you can see the angel inside,
even though you wonder who's in control when they are awake.
Give them a present and they'll play with the box ten times more.

In our world today of technology
and fast paces, we really owe it to ourselves,
to remember the happiness of the simple things for our children,
Like having a lollipop together while
you look for rainbows after a storm.

REMEMBER — Jobs will come and jobs will go,
But children are our treasures, enjoy them as they grow.

"Be of good courage, and he shall strengthen your heart, all ye that hope in the Lord."

Psalm 31:24

Raising Parents

My parents brought me home today, now it's my chance,
To show them just how much I know.

They thought they had it all figured out, they knew what to do,
But now we'll really see who's in control.

Their schedules were worked out, 8-5 work and 10-6 sleep,
Boy, I'm going to change everything.

I'll have them walking the floor all hours of the night,
And lullabies to me they will sing.

I started school today and mom was in tears,
She drove me to the front door.

Now I'm a teenager, with boyfriends and new clothes,
Mom says she can't see my floor.

I got my temps today and dad took me driving,
You can't imagine the look on his face.

I thought I was doing well, then that car got in my way,
Dad was saying prayers of thanks.

I'm graduating tomorrow and I can see it's been hard on them,
My parents sure learned some lessons though.

They've really developed well and they still remember back,
To when I was tiny and just starting to grow.

I'll be starting college soon, I'll call them for money and support,
But I'll really just be checking in.

You know, raising parents these days is really quite a chore,
They're determined to never give in.

"As an eagle stirreth up her nest, fluttereth over her young, spreadeth abroad her wings, taketh them, beareth them on her wings: So the Lord alone did lead him, and there was no strange god with him."

Deuteronomy 32:11-12

Booties In My Cereal

I had a picture perfect plan,
Of what my life would be,
A wonderful husband, great career,
And eventually a small family.

But the best laid plans,
Don't always work out,
When we heard that I was expecting,
We wanted to jump and shout.

The day we became parents,
We were brought to the reality,
That parenting entailed a whole lot more,
Than we ever thought there would be.

My husband and I had a juggling act,
That became our morning routine,
Trying to get ready for the day,
Without forgetting a thing.

Each morning the baby kick his booties off into my cereal,
We went though outfits because of spit-up and dirty pants,
But we learned that it's all part of family life,
And you have to laugh when you get the chance.

Now that our children are grown,
We have to chuckle when we think back,
You can't get stressed over the little things,
In reality it's only a short term act!

"Train up a child in the way he should go: and when he is old, he will not depart from it."

Proverbs 22:6

Military Mom

She raised us with "Tough Love" and she wears many hats,
She's one tough lady that takes nothing from brats!

She will lay down the law, yet capture your heart,
She will not put up with lying, so don't even start.

She can look you in the eyes, but see deep into your soul,
She can read children like a book, and she's got some mighty goals.

When dealing with mouthy kids, she can put them in their place,
She's not afraid of any teen and will get right in their face.

When we were young we soon learned just where we stood,
Consequences for being bad, rewards for being good.

She would not back down when we wanted things our way,
And when something needed to be done, she meant — NOW, TODAY!

I always thought that she was strict and expected way too much,
But as I grew, I soon realized, she did it out of love.

As I watch other families each going their own way,
I'm really glad that she is there to care for me each day.

She was never in the service, but she sure gets my salute,
She was nicknamed "Military Mom" and she really fit the boots.

"For he shall give his angels charge over thee, to keep thee in all thy ways."

Psalm 91:11

Tiny Angel Wings

Nine months of waiting, anticipation mighty great,
I carried you inside my womb, wanting to hold you close.

I would feel you stretch and kick, and then you'd do a somersault.
You were awake when I wanted to sleep, now I miss that most.

I loved to sing you lullabies, as I rubbed my stomach so soft.
Then you would settle down, as I rocked you with great care.

I marveled at your little face, tiny nose and rosy cheeks.
Counted each finger and toe, to make sure they were all there.

Then something happened, something went terribly wrong.
At first I blamed myself and cried, until I couldn't shed another tear.

As time went on I realized, that God needed you more than me.
So now I have to be strong, and give you up my dear.

He picked a little angel, a perfect one with a heart of gold.
He has a special job for you, he'll fit you with tiny angel wings.

You will be there to watch over children, in their hours of need.
To hold them close and keep them safe, comfort you will bring.

I'll miss you with all my heart, but God needs you now.
He has great plans for you, my child, to pass on His love.

And when my time is through on earth, I hope to carry me home,
You'll be the one to join the Lord, and take me to above.

"He hath made his wonderful works to be remembered:
the Lord is gracious and full of compassion."

Psalm 111:4

To Catch A Butterfly

People are always scurrying around,
Rushing here and rushing there.
Trying to catch a plane or train,
Hurrying everywhere.

The time is going so fast,
Minutes ticking away.
Meetings every hour,
Packing so much in each day.

The more people have in life,
The more they have to do.
Having so much pressure,
Can make a person blue.

Achieving that highest goal,
Is foremost on their minds.
Many forget about the ways,
To sit down and unwind.

Are they happy? You would think,
With all the toys they've got.
But by the time they can enjoy them,
Their energy is shot.

I've found that the greatest pleasures,
Can be found when we simply stop!
To catch a little butterfly,
You must sit down in one spot.

She'll flutter all about you,
And you'll marvel at her wings.
Your heart and eyes will dance,
You'll thank God for such a thing.

Oh, life will go on around you,
But for those few minutes that day,
You won't have a care in the world.
No one can steal that away.

You'll learn, the older you get,
That when pressures are building high,
You can unwind by sitting in a quiet field,
And teaching your children to catch a butterfly!

"And Jesus called a little child unto him, and set him in the midst of them, Whosoever therefore shall humble himself as this little child, the same is greatest in the kingdom of heaven."

Matthew 18:2,4

A Successful Tour Of Duty!

Success is ... rearranging your schedule to care for your sick child.

Success is ... the excitement in your child's eyes when they find out that you are NOT going to work that day, so you can watch their performance at school.

Success is ... watching your child beam when you bring their project to school that they forgot.

Success is ... taking the time to stop between appointments and help out in the classroom.

Success is ... your children bringing friends home after school, because other parents had to work late and you don't!

Success is ... being called "Military Mom," because you are always around to see what your children are up to and keep them in line.

Success is ... doing a family night once a week and your teenagers still think it's great.

Success is ... having your children take care of you when you are sick, because you were always there to take care of them.

Success is ... watching the lessons that are "caught" by your kids as they grow up.

Success is ... having your kids give you a funny card, because *YOU* need a pick-me-up.

Success is ... the lessons your family learns from you not allowing the word **"QUIT"!**

Success is ... having your kids tell you that your LOVE was the best present you could give them!

Success is ... having your children say "Thanks for being so tough," when they are at home with you and someone they know is sitting in jail.

Success is ... having your children tell you that they learned more about life from the tough times, than when you handed things to them.

Success is ... seeing the positive attitude your children have towards others because of what they've learned from you.

Success is ... telling your children "I'm Proud of You" for the small accomplishments in their life.

Success is ... having your grown children tell you "Thanks" for keeping the family PRIORITIES in order.

Success is ... Committing to the Tour of Duty to be a Parent!

"ARISE, shine; for thy light is come, and the glory of the Lord is risen upon thee. For, behold, the darkness shall cover the earth, and gross darkness the people: but the Lord shall arise upon thee, and his glory shall be seen upon thee."

Isaiah 60:1-2

TINY — The Little Snowflake Who Wouldn't QUIT!
(Written for children with Myasthenia Gravis and all those battling childhood illnesses.)

Tiny was the smallest snowflake, fragile in many ways,
But Tiny was determined to always enjoy his days.

He wasn't going to give in to all this falling stuff,
He spent his days among the clouds, to prove that he was tough.

As he watched the older snowflakes, lay softly on the ground,
Tiny decided he was different, and wasn't floating down.

He was going to gather all his strength, and stay up in the sky,
For his positive look at life, would keep him flying high.

He connected with other little snowflakes, and together they agreed,
The cold wind couldn't blow them down, there was much for them to see.

So hand in hand they formed a chain, a link so mighty tight,
They would help each other on tough days, so they could stay in flight.

As Tiny started getting tired, his muscles getting weak,
The others held him up, and gave the encouragement he'd seek.

And in the small snowflake's life, it was really great to know,
That when the tough winds blow, there's always a place to go.

A special place for little snowflakes, like Tiny and his friends,
Where they can go and help each other, until the bad times end.

So when the going gets tough, stay determined and always smile.
To get your mind off your problems, just think of Tiny for a while.

He'll be dancing in the clouds, on the coldest days.
He won't let life get him down; he enjoys his time to play.

(For information on Myasthenia Gravis
please turn to the last page of this book.)

"I am the good shepherd, and know my sheep, and am known of mine. As the Father knoweth me, even so know I the Father: and I lay down my life for the sheep."

John 10:14-15

My Two Fathers

One father is a carpenter, a builder of dreams.
One father is a designer of landscaping scenes.

Together you've both been a shaper of my life.
You've taught me to be strong through all of my strife.

It's a common saying that "Love is not taught!"
The feelings of love can only be caught.

Love is caught through actions and deeds being done.
Love is caught in the laughter of people having fun.

Love is caught through the times of sharing from the heart.
Love is caught in my memories when we're apart.

Though in your lives you've been through tough times,
Having you both there for me was a comforting sign.

One thing you have taught me, one thing I hold dear,
Is that I could come to you both, when I had problems and fears.

You've both shaped my life, in so many ways,
You taught me to be strong and to try each day.

I thank each of you, from down in my heart,
For the love that you've given me right from the start.

Sometimes in words, "Love" is hard to say.
But you both showed me your love in so many ways.

So I thank my father, my builder of dreams.
And I thank my other father, of landscaping scenes.

"For his anger endureth but a moment; in his favour is life: weeping may endure for a night, but joy cometh in the morning."

Psalm 30:5

What A.D.D. Children Will Add To Your Life

They wake up in the morning and start to bounce like rubber balls.
They wiggle here and giggle there.

They have an energy that never stops, questioning everything in their path.
They are full of motion and have a passion for life.

They can wear most people out in a small amount of time,
And their focus for any task is short.

These are the children with Attention
Deficit Disorder, and as a parent I know,
They will ADD great things to your life, if you will take time to notice.

But sometimes, as adults, we are too busy to pay attention,
To really work with that child and to find out what makes them tick.

We want everyone to run on our schedule and do things on our time.
These children have their own time frame and need much love.

They will notice things we've overlooked, every noise will turn their head.
Every item is a must for their collections and they have many.

Their rooms are in disarray, homework is a chore to get done,
But every commercial or video game will hold their interest.

They need to be moving all the time.
Their joy for life will capture your heart and bring you to tears.

They can be tough to deal with and have excuses for everything,
As parents we need to be tougher, yet show more love than ever.

They will try your patience to the last degree, don't pull your hair out yet,
Because as they get older, you will look back and realize with great relief,

That's it's not what you TAUGHT them that's important,
But what you CAUGHT from each other that will make it all worthwhile.

They caught your love. You caught their joy for adventure.
They caught your trust. You caught their sense of humor.
They caught your belief in them. You caught their energy for living.

Yes, I can truly say that A.D.D. children will ADD more to
your life than you will ever know.
ENJOY THE JOURNEY TOGETHER!

"Blessed are the pure in heart: for they shall see God."
Matthew 5:8

When You Can't Go To God's House

I grew up in a big family and on Sunday morn,
Getting everyone ready for church was a chore.

Mom got us all cleaned up and dressed,
Sat us down and said "Now, don't get a mess!"

We were five little girls, hats, gloves and all,
Always lined up from biggest to small.

One Sunday I got sick and started to cry,
As they all went to church, except Grandma and I.

I asked her "What will happen? Will God be mad?"
"I can't go to his house, will he think that I'm bad?"

Grandma smiled and said in her wise old way,
"Ask God to visit *your* house today."

I looked at her with surprise on my face,
I said "How do I ask Him to come to my place?"

She said "Put your hands together and open your heart,"
"And soon your visit with God will start."

I knelt by her side and closed my eyes,
Then I had a feeling that someone arrived.

I looked around and said "God, are you there?"
"I asked you to come, because I need care."

"I can't go to your house, I'm sick today,"
"So I asked you to come to visit and play."

"Would you like to play dress up or take dolls for a walk?"
He said "How about if we sit and just have a talk."

We sat down together at my table and chairs,
He had a warm smile and his eyes showed He cared.

We talked there for hours, just God and I,
Then I gave Him a hug as He said "Good-bye."

I thanked Him and said "What a great day it's been."
He replied "Call me anytime. I'll come visit again."

"Create in me a clean heart, O God; and renew a right spirit within me."

Psalm 51:10

Those Old Shoes

Children often play a game, it's really fun to do,
They sit around in a circle, and each takes off their shoes.

They throw them in the middle, then the game's begun,
They get to pick someone else's shoes, and spend a day in them for fun.

The first time that I played the game, I remember the lesson I got,
Was that the life of others, wasn't as wonderful as I thought.

I got to take my pick first, because I had the oldest shoes,
Mine were always hand me down, so I picked some that were brand new.

As I put those shoes on, I felt something strange inside,
They made it hard for me to walk, my feet twisted to the side.

The little girl who owned these shoes, wore braces to her knees.
She was born with bones deformed, these helped build muscles in her feet.

I spent a day in those shoes, they were beautiful, that's so true.
But I was glad to get my old pair back,
Even though the soles were wearing through.

The lesson that I've learned from that game,
Stays with me until this day.
When you think that someone's life is so great,
Put on their shoes and walk their way.

"And there were in the same country shepherds abiding in the field, keeping watch over their flock by night. And, lo, the angel of the Lord came upon them, and the glory of the Lord shone round about them: and they were sore afraid. And the angel said onto them, Fear not: for, behold, I bring you good tidings of great joy, which shall be to all people. For unto you is born this day in the city of David a Saviour, which is Christ the Lord. And this shall be a sign unto you; Ye shall find the babe wrapped in swaddling clothes, lying in a manger. And suddenly there was with the angel a multitude of the heavenly host praising God, and saying, Glory to God in the highest, and on earth peace, goodwill toward men."

Luke 2:8-14

Please Put Christ Back In Christmas

Please put Christ back in Christmas and remember all the love,
Of what this day should mean to us and whom we should think of,
It's of giving not receiving, giving all the love we can,
Of all the gifts we've received from that Special Man.

The kids came in the other day, said "Mom, here's our list!"
"We've written down the things we want for this Christmas."
"Commercials say these are the best toys out this year,"
"And, Mom, we want them so bad, we'll cry if they're not here!"

The kids and I sat down to talk on that very day.
I realized we looked at Christmas in our separate ways.
I told them of the Christ Child and of his strife,
Of all the things He gave for us, including his own life.

A week's gone by now and my kids came in with their new list,
Of all the people they could help for this Christmas,
Saying "Mom, we don't need anything, we've got so much you know,"
"We want to give to others to help the Lord's love grow."

On Christmas Day the kids saw the gifts beneath the tree.
They thanked us ahead of time, for whatever they might be,
Then they had a special request, it made me shed a tear,
They gave their gifts to others less fortunate that year.

The tears came to my eyes, my heart it swelled with pride.
My kids put Christ back in Christmas, their own wants on the side.
This Christmas will stay forever in my mind.
Putting Christ back in Christmas spreads love to all mankind.

Please put Christ back in Christmas and remember all the love,
Of what this day should mean to us and whom we should think of,
It's of giving not receiving, giving all the love we can,
Of all the gifts we've received from that Special Man.

"I waited patiently for the Lord; and he inclined unto me, and heard my cry. He brought me up also out of an horrible pit, out of the miry clay, and set my feet upon a rock, and established my goings."

Psalm 40:1-2

CHAPTER 3

Watch Out ... For Those Ruts!

"Be careful for nothing; but in every thing by prayer and supplication with thanksgiving let your requests be made known unto God. And the peace of God, which passeth all understanding, shall keep your hearts and minds through Christ Jesus."

Philippians 4:6-7

Bootstraps

When I was young, I was always at the stable,
I loved to trot the horses around.
Then one day my horse was spooked,
And bucked me to the ground.

The owner, an old cowboy, started to laugh.
He said "You've just learned a lesson for life!"
"When you get bucked off, grab your bootstraps,"
"Pick yourself back up and ride."

I got up, but I was sure angry!
I didn't realize what that cowboy meant.
But as I grew older, that lesson learned,
Stayed in my mind like cement.

Now when things go wrong and hard knocks happen,
As we all know quite often they can,
I grab my bootstraps and pick myself up,
I've learned to take my stand.

Throughout the years those leather straps,
Have been used quite a lot.
But they remind me, the thinner they get,
Of the determination I have got.

So next time you take a blow,
And you find yourself sitting on the ground,
Pick yourself up, dust yourself off,
And turn your situation around.

"The Lord is my light and my salvation; whom shall I
fear? the Lord is the strength of my life; of whom shall I
be afraid?"

Psalm 27:1

Don't Drive On The Sidewalk!

I was driving through life, doing mighty fine.
Everything was going great, until I saw that sign.
It was in great big letters, I knew just what it said,
ROAD UNDER CONSTRUCTION — DETOUR AHEAD!

I started to look around, to see which way to go,
Looking left and right, this road I did not know.
I was getting in a panic, because I didn't have a map.
I was growing very tired, I really needed to take a nap.

People driving here and there, nowhere to stop and talk,
In my confusion, next thing I knew, I was driving on the walk.
Now dodging poles and people, it really wasn't nice.
Why does everything have to be, such a mess in my life?

I finally got my car stopped, unpeeled my hands from the wheel.
Boy, I hated detours! They're such a traumatic deal!
People were looking at me, as if I'd lost my mind.
Then I looked up and saw a man, his eyes they seemed so kind.

He walked over to my window, and asked "Are you lost?"
"Not knowing where you're going, can be dangerous at any cost."
I told him that I was on the detour, and simply went astray.
He said "Let's spend some time together,
And you can get on with your day."

I decided to take a break, and talk with him for awhile.
He had the nicest eyes, and the warmest smile.
He asked me what happened? What upset me so?
I said "I hate when there are detours, and I don't know where to go."

He told me "In the journey of life, getting from here to there,"
You will always find things in your path, detours everywhere."
"You must use your head and think things out just right,"
"And when your road seems the darkest, always look for my light."

I was staring at the ground just then, when I glanced up he was gone,
But He left me with that message, and I knew where I went wrong.
I got back in my car, and drove it off the walk.
Now when I'm faced with detours, I know with Jesus I can talk.

"But thou, O Lord, art a shield for me; my glory, and the lifter up of mine head. I cried unto the Lord with my voice, and he heard me out of his holy hill. Se'lah. I laid me down and slept; I awaked; for the Lord sustained me."

Psalm 3:3-5

I Asked God ... "Why?"

I had a dream one night, that I got to meet GOD,
In his mansion in the sky.
I had many questions, I wanted some answers,
So I simply asked GOD ... "WHY?"

He said, "Come my child, sit with me."
And He gently took my hand.
We walked through the clouds and sat down by His throne,
I thought He'd show me His plan.

As He started to speak, I knew He'd reveal,
Just what was on His mind.
I sat there and listened, with great anticipation,
I would finally get answers to.... WHY?

The message He gave me was so profound,
I sat back and gave Him a stare.
He said, "My child, we needed to talk,"
"I gave you struggles, because I care."

"It's not in the good times, but in the trials of life,"
"That's when I'm calling you out."
"I hoped that you'd listen and stop what you're doing,"
"But sometimes I just have to shout!"

"I needed your attention, I love you my dear,"
"I have so much I wanted to say,"
"But you were too busy, you left me out,"
"When I throw struggles in, then you pray."

"The lines are now open and we can speak,"
"Our communication can start,"
"When you are down on your knees and give me your attention,"
"We can talk straight from the heart."

"So when things go wrong and life gets tough,"
"There might be something I need,"
"Pause for a moment, listen for my voice,"
"I want you to talk with me."

"When you have questions and want to know why,"
"Please take some time to stop!"
"I'm always here, to help you out,"
"But remember it gets lonely at the TOP!"

"But if we hope for that we see not, then do we with patience wait for it. And we know that all things work together for good to them that love God, to them who are the called according to his purpose."

Romans 8:25,28

A Special Plan

She lived in her own little world,
She was different from you and me.
But God had a plan for her,
We always wondered what it would be.

Though she was mentally challenged,
She was as lively as she could be.
She lived to the age of 72,
But her development had stopped at three.

Many would ask "What's her purpose in life?"
"Why does she have to live this way?"
But God knew His plan for her,
Would be revealed to us some day.

She had a passion to live in happiness,
Until the day her life came to an end.
But that was just the beginning,
Of what was in God's special plan.

On that day a decision was made,
To pass on her joy for life,
A decision to donate her organs,
To help others win their fight.

The love for life that she showed us,
We understood her the best we can,
Now her spirit will live on in others,
For that was God's Special Plan!

"Wait on the Lord: be of good courage, and he shall strengthen thine heart: wait, I say, on the Lord."

Psalm 27:14

The Weight Off My Mind

I always wanted to be thin,
And boy I worked like mad,
To watch each bite I took,
And exercise every chance I had.

I met a lady with the opposite problem,
She couldn't put on any weight,
No matter how much she tried,
Or how much food she ate.

Our problems were similar,
Though at first neither of us could see,
Because we were both so stressed out,
Thinking of only "Me!"

Then we decided to do volunteer work,
To care for people who needed some help.
We started thinking of others,
Instead of thinking of just ourselves.

We were sharing life with people who were dying,
And though their time was going fast,
We'd talk with them and tell a few jokes,
Sometimes we would all crack up and laugh.

That was the greatest diet we had,
Because the weight was off our minds.
We found out what's most important in life,
Is not our size, but the LOVE we carry inside.

"If my people, which are called by my name, shall humble themselves, and pray, and seek my face, and turn from their wicked ways, then will I hear from heaven, and will forgive their sin, and will heal their land."

2 Chronicles 7:14

Where's The Control?

As He walked around the heavenly clouds,
God was looking high and low,
Asking all the angels
If they had seen His control?

The angels seemed a bit confused,
And didn't know which way to go,
They went to the saints and asked
"Have you seen God's control?"

The saints were really perplexed at this,
"Was it the control for the television or DVD?"
They looked by God's favorite chair,
But where could it be?

God was keeping calm and cool,
Though everyone was ripping the heavens apart,
Finally a little angel said "When all else fails,
Go back to the start!"

So everyone went back into God's living room,
And started looking under tables and chairs,
They found all of the remotes and
then gave God a funny stare.

"O.K. Lord, what's going on?"
"The remotes have all been found."
God said with a bewildered look
"The control I've lost is on the ground!"

"No one gives me a thought these days,"
"But once their lives get out of line,"
"They beg and ask for help,
And then they want my attention all the time."

Everyone in heaven gave a sigh,
They looked at God and totally agreed,
He's lost control of His people and
More prayers are what they need.

Remember this little story,
Next time you are hunting for your keys or the remote,
Stop and give some time to God;
Let Him know He's still in control.

"Hear me, O Lord, hear me, that this people may know that thou art the Lord God, and that thou hast turned their heart back again."

1 Kings 18:37

It's All In How You Look At Life

I broke a nail, my nylons ran,
My day is just falling apart,
I'm running late, the kids are pokey,
Now my car won't start.

I have a cold, my nose is drippy,
Why is this happening to me?
I have a meeting and no one cares,
Just how tired I am getting to be.

I went to the doctor and was telling him,
"I feel so sick I could gag."
Then I walked out of his office and saw a little girl,
Who was there with no legs.

My problems seemed so big 'til that point,
Then I was put in my place,
I was thinking of how bad I felt,
Until I saw her smiling face.

I realized it's all in how we look at life,
That gives us the strength to get through,
So now when I'm feeling low,
I think of what others have to do.

I may have a cold, a drippy nose,
Or something that can ruin my day,
But others go on, much worse off than me,
And smile some how, some way.

I don't let the little things bother me,
And I've learned to smile so much more,
We all have to endure some hard times in life,
Only God knows what's in store.

Life Is Like A Stream
by: Jennifer Renderman

Life is like a stream,
You never know where it will go,
You never know what rocks it will hit,
You never know who will step in it,
Sometimes they are long,
Sometimes they are short.
Life is like a stream.

CHAPTER 4

The Courage To Journey On

"Sing, O heavens; and be joyful, O earth; and break forth into singing, O mountains: for the Lord hath comforted his people, and will have mercy upon his afflicted."

Isaiah 49:13

Snowflakes

*(Dedicated to patients around the world with Myasthenia
Gravis. MG is a neuromuscular disorder that affects each person
so differently, they call it a "Snowflake" disease.)*

MG'ers are like the Snowflakes,
All unique - you will agree,
MG is something that affects us,
Each so differently!

The Snowflakes, no two alike,
Are special in many ways,
They're delicate, but yet so strong,
And they dance on the coldest days.

And like the Snowflakes that land together,
In the sun they seem to shine,
MG'ers give hope to each other,
To get through the toughest times.

May this Snowflake remind you,
When it comes to call,
That our thoughts and prayers are sent,
To give you courage through it all.

Blessings for better days!

(For information about Myasthenia Gravis
please turn to the last page of this book.)

"The Lord is my strength and my shield; my heart trusted in him, and I am helped: therefore my heart greatly rejoiceth; and with my song will I praise him."

Psalm 28:7

An Angel On Wheels

(With special thanks to Renée Bondi and her music ministry.)

Her voice is that of an ANGEL,
Singing encouragement and praise,
Of the guidance that God gives us,
To help us through tough days.

Her face it beams so brightly,
Her eyes sparkle and shine,
Though she can't walk, she helps others,
To know that God will be there in the worst of times.

In her songs, she passes on His message,
Of the great things that God can do.
She's an inspiration of His presence,
And that He's created a "good work" in you.

Though she doesn't have use of her legs,
Her determination and faith aren't disguised,
She's a "Never Quit - Angel on Wheels,"
With the Lord right by her side.

So I thank her from deep in my heart,
She's shown me through her ways,
That a disability doesn't have to stop us in life,
God will give us strength to build better days.

"And he shall be like a tree planted by the rivers of water,
that bringeth forth his fruit in his season; his leaf also
shall not wither; and whatsoever he doeth shall prosper."
.
Psalm 1:3

The Golden River

From the mountains up so high,
Through the valleys beneath the sky,
The river comes traveling down,
With the flow of a gentle, soothing sound.

Trickling over stones so lightly,
Or shining in the sun so brightly,
The river's tune fills my ears,
A sound of peace that calms my fears.

The river is also nourishment to life,
The water never stops, day or night,
It provides life for the fish and the trees,
Without water we'd all go to our knees.

While lying in my hospital bed,
With the IV dripping overhead,
I close my eyes and listen to the sound,
I picture a golden river running down.

I think of this liquid flowing into my veins,
Like a river being refilled during the gentle rains.
Without being replenished it would simply go dry,
And the life it provides would surely die.

This liquid is sustaining my life,
It may make me nauseous, but I need it to fight,
It's killing the cells that are taking me down,
So I lie back and relax, as I listen to the sound.

I may feel sick and for a while I'll be weak,
But I fight on today, for it's my future I seek.
So as I lie there I begin to pray,
I ask God for strength to get me through the day.

I feel a hand on my shoulder, so warm and so strong,
Giving me the courage to help me go on.
I open my eyes, but no one is there,
Then I knew God was by my side to give me His care.

"Have mercy upon me, O Lord; for I am weak: O Lord, heal me; for my bones are vexed."

Psalm 6:2

Don't Be A Pain

Pain hits us all and even the tough can become,
Wimpy and whiny to the end.
But don't fall into that trap and you'll be better off,
For a smile can build lots of friends.

I know what it's like, I've endured pain all my life,
And I can tell you from experience it's true,
Whether it's an injury, or surgery, an infection or a bug,
Feeling miserable can make you blue.

But Grandma gave me advice, in her wise old way,
That has made a difference in my life,
Always smile when you really don't want to,
And always treat other people nice.

We see doctors and nurses when we're usually in pain,
And we might feel just a little off.
But it lessens that pain and makes others feel good,
Even if our smile is soft.

A smile releases endorphins to get through the pain,
It can even help you have a little fun,
So try to smile and be nice, even if you hurt,
And remember when you're in pain - Don't Be One!

"Hear, O Lord, and have mercy upon me: Lord, be thou my helper. Thou hast turned for me my mourning into dancing: thou hast put off my sackcloth, and girded me with gladness;"

Psalm 30:10-11

What I Thought I've Lost In Life...

I've Actually Found I've Gained!

The life that I once knew, has now been taken away.
A medical condition, has slowed me down each day.

This trial placed before me, has put me in much pain,
But what I thought I lost in life, I've actually found I've gained.

People often ask me, "How can you smile through each day?"
I say "It's how you look at life," and I go on my merry way.

Yes, I've lost the use of muscles, I was always on the go,
But now I see the things I've missed, because I travel slow.

I was irritated by traffic, people always in my way,
Now I use the time I'm stopped, to meditate and pray.

I felt like I was missing things, working morning until night,
Now I listen to the birds, and gaze up at the starry light.

I would rush the kids to school, to get on with my busy day,
Now I cherish every moment, that I can sit and watch them play.

I was always running about, rushing here and rushing there,
Now I've time to spend with friends, and lend a hand to show I care.

My thoughts were always consumed, planning the next big event,
Now they are filled with special people, I thank God for those He sent.

I have wonderful friends and family, who support me through it all,
So I've learned to make the most of life, joke around and have a ball.

I believe God places challenges, in our path so He can see,
If we're going to sit around and mope, or be as happy as we can be.

For the things I thought I've lost in life, I wanted to sit and mourn,
But I've actually found that I've gained,
A whole lot more than I had before.

"The Lord upholdeth all that fall, and raiseth up all those that be bowed down. The eyes of all wait upon thee; and thou givest them their meat in due season."

Psalm 145:14-15

Rise Above It All!

My battles in life were many,
Struggles seemed to make it a long haul,
But I want you to remember one thing,
I ROSE ABOVE IT ALL!

Disasters, sickness and surgeries,
I don't know why I had to deal with it all,
I asked for God's hand, He lifted me up,
I ROSE ABOVE IT ALL!

I started each day with a special prayer,
"God, help me answer your call."
I asked for His help to guide me through,
I ROSE ABOVE IT ALL!

He blessed me with special people,
They knew I had to laugh through it all,
I thanked God for sending them when I needed a lift,
To help me RISE ABOVE IT ALL!

So try to remember how Jesus lived,
Get up each time you have a fall,
Smile through the tough times and laugh through the pain,
And you too will — RISE ABOVE IT ALL!

"How beautiful upon the mountains are the feet of him that bringeth good tidings, that publisheth peace; that bringeth good tidings of good, that publisheth salvation; that saith unto Zion, Thy God reigneth!"

Isaiah 52:7

The MOUNtain

(With special thanks to Drs. Robert H. and Robert A. Schuller, of the Crystal Cathedral Ministries. Their positive "Hour of Power" messages have helped me realize that Tough Times Never Last and there is always away Over, Under, Around or
Through every mountain in life!)

As I stood before my mountain, overcome with fear, I cried!
I tried to see the top of it, but it reached far into the sky.

"Where do I begin?" I thought, "Do I have the strength to even start?"
Then I remembered a minister's message, it put hope into my heart.

"Tough Times Never Last," he said, "But Tough People Do!"
So I gave my fears to God, my belief it really grew.

I started to climb my mountain, with each step came great pain,
I knew that God would give me strength, so I prayed as I climbed again.

Half way up the mountain, I looked out and saw the sights,
Now all the clouds were lifting, an eagle was in flight.

The view from here was clearer now, the top not far away,
Excitement rushed through my soul, again to God I prayed.

"Dear Lord, thank you, for giving me this feat!"
"Once I've conquered my mountain, this challenge will be complete."

As I face the struggles of life, each and every day,
I know the Lord will guide me, over the obstacles in my way.

I will not become discouraged, on with life I'll go!
With each mountain that I overcome, the stronger I will grow.

When I finally reach the top, the one thing that I shall do,
Is look around and find someone, who needs help up too.

Together we will stand, on the mountaintop and pray,
And thank God for the challenges, that make us grow each day.

"The people that walked in darkness have seen a great light: they that dwell in the land of the shadow of death, upon them hath the light shined."

Isaiah 9:2

CHAPTER 5

A Light In The Dark

"And when he was come into the house, the blind men came to him: and Jesus saith unto them, Believe ye that I am able to do this? They said unto him, Yea, Lord. Then touched he their eyes, saying According to your faith be it unto you. And their eyes were opened;"

Matthew 9:28-30

Blind Faith

I met a man who could not see and I was surprised at what he said,
Though he was totally blind he could describe things in his head.

I asked him how he pictured this beautiful summer day?
He said the sun was shining bright and he heard birds out to play.

I asked him what it was like to walk along the river's path?
He said the trail was beautiful and the flowers were blooming fast.

I asked what it was like to cross the busy city streets?
He said that people were in a hurry and weren't pleasant on that beat.

I asked if he could describe the mountains that reached up so high?
He said those were God's building stones to help us reach the sky.

I asked him if he knew when the weather was going to change?
He said he felt moisture in the air when it's about to rain.

I asked how he could believe in things when he didn't have his sight?
He said that he had more faith than people who see in the light.

He went on to explain that having sight could cause great fear,
People must live with blind faith and know that God is always near.

You learn a special trust when you let God guide your way.
You learn to make the best of life and enjoy every day.

You learn who you can count on to lend you a hand.
You learn that having less is more and that God has a special plan.

When you can't see what you're missing, maybe it's not important at all,
For what we really need in life, God will provide it all.

This special man became my friend and now that he is gone,
He left me with his message of *Blind Faith* to live on.

"HEAR me when I call, O God of my righteousness: thou hast enlarged me when I was in distress; have mercy upon me, and hear my prayer."

Psalm 4:1

An Elephant On My Head!

I've prayed all my life and when trouble sets in,
I ask God to give me a sign,
Sometimes His answers are in the smallest form,
So I've learned to open my mind.

I asked God one time to give me some peace,
And he sent me a butterfly,
But I was too busy rushing through the day,
I didn't notice and it simply flew by.

I told God again that I needed a sign,
My life was so full of stress,
This time he sent a squirrel to visit,
But all I saw was his mess.

I begged God "Please, I need a BIG sign today,"
"Before I wind up dead!"
In His sense of humor to slow me down,
He placed an elephant on my head.

Now that I'm stopped completely flat,
I have time to think this one out,
How do I remove this pressure from my life,
When I can't even shout?

"O.K. Lord, you've got my attention!"
"On this one you really came through,"
"Next time I need a *BIG* sign in my life,"
"I'll simply bring my problems to YOU!"

"For thou hast been a strength to the poor, a strength to the needy in his distress, a refuge from the storm, a shadow from the heat, when the blast of the terrible ones is as a storm against the wall."

Isaiah 25:4

Give It All To God

The clouds are building over head,
A storm is brewing mighty big,
The branches on my tree of life,
Are being tossed about like twigs.

The thunder rings through my ears,
The wind it starts to whip,
I try to hang on through the gusts of rain,
But it overpowers my grip.

I feel the pain so great,
As I fall and hit the ground,
The lightening bolts are everywhere,
Cracking all around.

I pray to God that this tree of mine,
Can withstand this mighty storm,
I know all seems darkest now,
And will be brighter in the morn.

In the dawning light of day,
I can see it all so clear,
When the storm seemed the worst, I gave it all to God,
For with Him I have nothing to fear.

"When the waves of death compassed me, the floods of ungodly men made me afraid; the sorrows of hell compassed me about; the snares of death prevented me; In my distress I called upon the Lord, and cried to my God: and he did hear my voice out of his temple, and my cry did enter into his ears. God is my strength and power: and he maketh my way perfect."

2 Samuel 22: 5-7,33

God's Beacon Of Light!

The sea is rough, waves crash about,
Which way to go, I have much doubt.

This vessel of mine, being tossed to and fro,
There's no turning back, so onward I go.

The night is dark, rain pouring down,
Fear growing stronger, what if I'd drown.

I fall to my knees, holding the wheel,
"God, help me through," I make my appeal.

He's always there, in the tough times of life,
"Please show me the way, show me the light!"

Rain hits my eyes, it's hard to see,
Then a flash of light, hits the choppy sea.

Again I see a light, bouncing around,
I know land is near, I'll soon be on ground.

That lighthouse light, like a God-sent friend,
Will help me get home, safely again.

Though the storms in my life, may make me fear,
I know God's Beacon of Light, will always be near.

"Also I heard the voice of the Lord, saying, Whom shall I
send, and who will go for us? Then said I, Here am I;
send me."

Isaiah 6:8

The Edge Of Time

I was standing on the cliff, watching the waves crash to the shore,
Money was low, debts were high, and I couldn't go on any more.

I had reached the point of depression, I was totally in despair,
I thought that jumping was my answer out, I didn't think anyone cared.

While I stood out on that ledge, a cold sweat came over me,
I was frozen on the edge of time, just wanting to be free.

I looked up toward the heavens, and cried out into the sky,
"Why does life hurt so much?" I wanted to jump and die.

Suddenly from out of nowhere, a great wind started to blow,
It knocked me to the ground, I sat there with no place to go.

Then just as quick as it started, the wind became so calm,
I heard a voice call my name, it said "You're needed, you must go on!"

I looked around for someone, but no one knew I was there,
Again I heard that voice saying, "I love you, I'll always care!"

I stood up and looked all around, I called "Please show your face."
Who could be talking to me, in this high and lonely place?

Now for just a few minutes, my troubles seemed to disappear,
I felt a sense of peace, it helped to calm my fears.

I sat down once more, and looked toward the heavens so great,
I asked "God is that you? Did you save me from this fate?"

"If I am supposed to go on, please tell me why."
Then I saw an eagle overhead, it was soaring up in the sky.

I knew that this was my answer, so I said "God, please take my hand,"
"If you can use me to help others, Lord - here I am!"

That was the day that changed my life, though at first I didn't believe,
That there was a God who even cared, now I praise Him on bended knees!

"In the day of prosperity be joyful, but in the day of adversity consider: God also hath set the one over against the other, to the end that man should find nothing after him."

Ecclesiastes 7:14

The Tornado

"I've never seen anything like it before,"
The people were saying as they came out of their doors,
They were disheartened as they started looking around,
At all the debris spread over the ground.

The warning sirens were so few,
But when I saw that black cloud I knew,
Something bad was heading this way,
We must take shelter in a very safe place.

The tornado came and went so fast,
It left destruction throughout its path.
All we saw as we opened the door,
Was that we didn't have much left anymore.

Our entire area was wiped out,
You could hear sobbing from people about,
But we didn't know what was in store,
That God was watching with plans galore.

He showed us through our strife,
We had more than belongings, we still had our lives,
He scooped up the pieces and turned them about,
He showed us that loving people would help out.

People giving of themselves to show they cared,
Neighbors helping neighbors were everywhere,
Folks going around saying "What can I do?"
Strangers pitching in while saying "How do you do!"

When disasters hit we think "What will it cost,"
"To replace all the items that we have lost?"
It sometimes takes a tragedy to find out what's left,
How much life really means and how we've been blessed.

So when things go wrong take them in stride,
Remember it's all small stuff in the journey of life,
Take time each day to give praise and thanks,
For what God has blessed you with, you can't keep in the banks.

"Then they cry unto the Lord in their trouble, and he bringeth them out of their distresses. He maketh the storm a calm, so that the waves thereof are still."

Psalm 107:28-29

Tie A Knot And Let Go

When all is going wrong and you seemed so confused,
They say "Tie a knot at the end of your rope and don't let go."
But I have a saying that gives more hope,
"Tie a knot and give God the controls!"

I ask Him to help me and He holds out His hands,
I can feel Him catching me as I am falling,
I have strayed off the path and I need His light,
I can hear His voice, my name He is calling.

Who knows better what I need in my life?
He is always there when I take the time,
On the bleakest of nights when all feels lost,
I realize His vision is better than mine.

At first I wasn't sure if He heard us,
But He listens if we are willing to share,
He will pick us up and set us on the right path,
And give His love to show that He cares.

Now it's our turn to do a good deed for God,
Let others know what He has done in our life,
Lend a helping hand, listen with a caring ear,
And pass on His light to brighten someone's night.

"The angel of the Lord encampeth round about them that fear him, and delivereth them."

Psalm 34:7

CHAPTER 6

Traveling With ... Wings, Prayers And Companions

"But the path of the just is as the shining light, that shineth more and more unto the perfect day."

Proverbs 4:18

The Vacation

We had planned it for months, we knew where we were going to go,
We were heading south, where there wasn't any snow!

Our money had been saved, we counted every cent,
Each stop was mapped out, so our time would be well spent.

The car was loaded, excitement was running high,
It was a beautiful morning to start out, not a cloud up in the sky.

Friends said "We hope you have a good time,
Write us when you get there."
There was no "hope" about it,
We were going to have fun, and forget about our cares.

Half way to our destination, thunder started banging overhead,
It was hard to see where we were going, suddenly the road came to an end.

This wasn't on our map, I had called and checked it out,
The kids were scared and tired, I just wanted to shout.

Nothing in sight for miles, what do you do when the road just quits?
Do we turn around and go back home, or do we continue on with the trip?

With all the traveling that we had done, I wasn't turning around now,
I had to find another road, and go on with our journey somehow.

As I drove through that dark and rainy night,
I kept looking for some lights,
My mind was wandering and I started to think,
"This is really like our lives."

We spend time planning out, just what we think our futures will hold,
But when we're faced with road closings, do we stop or find a new road?

It took us longer to reach our destination, than I had ever planned,
But I've learned when the going gets tough,
You really have to take a stand.

We had to follow that same road home,
But this time it was by the light of day.
We were surprised at the scenery we would have missed,
If we had gone the original way.

We spend much time planning our lives,
And we think that we're in control,
But there comes a time when our plans will change,
And we must let God show us which way to go.

"Bear ye one another's burdens, and so fulfil the law of Christ. As we have therefore opportunity, let us do good unto all men, especially unto them who are of the household of faith."

Galatians 6:2,10

An Angel Who's Always There!

My precious friend you are so dear,
And I hope you know this comes from my heart,
I'm so glad you came into my life,
And that we didn't drift far apart.

You have walked with me down life's roads,
Through the good times and the bad,
I thank God every day for a friend like you,
A special angel when I'm sad.

Most people say they are friends all right,
But where are they when you need an ear?
You are on the phone or send a note,
To let me know that you are near.

Sometimes the days are terribly long,
And the nights seem even worse,
Then along comes your note to brighten my day,
With such a special verse.

I'd pick up the phone and hear your voice,
Because you were just checking in,
You'd tell me a story or crack a joke,
You can always make me grin.

The longer we'd talk the lighter the load,
And we'd begin to laugh,
You make me forget my problems,
Or the difficulties of the past.

Somehow time stops completely still,
When we have the chance to chat,
Whether it's deep in a conversation,
Or just about this and that.

When we hang up the phone my heart is warmed,
Because you showed you cared,
I thank God again for a friend like you,
An Angel Who's Always There!

"And he hath put a new song in my mouth, even praise unto our God: many shall see it, and fear, and shall trust in the Lord."

Psalm 40:3

Kindness Can Save A Life

People thought that I had it all,
    great job and nice cars,
But in reality my life was a mess,
    damaged by many scars.

I had reached the lowest point I could go,
    my marriage was on rocks,
I was really sinking fast, and at work,
    I felt like I was stuck in a box.

I didn't know how I was going to go on,
    I didn't know what to do,
I had reached the end of my rope,
    I wanted it all to be through.

This was going to be my last day on Earth,
    I was tired of all the pain,
I didn't care if I lived or died,
    I just wanted to be out of misery again.

I stopped at the store before I went home,
    I met a lady who said the kindest thing,
    "You've got the nicest smile,"
    her comment through my ears did ring.

I saw her again at the checkout,
she asked if she could get my name,
She said she was new to the area,
so our information we did exchange.

I sat in my car and thought "Now that was dumb,"
I was going to end it all that night,
But I went home in a better mood,
for once my husband and I didn't fight.

Around 8 p.m. the phone rang,
and I heard her familiar voice,
She asked if we could meet for coffee,
I knew I didn't have a choice.

We met for coffee and I found out,
that she had been in the same situation as mine,
She told me what she did to turn life around,
and how things got better over time.

I decided to change my life,
to look for support and get some help,
Now I give compliments to others who looked stressed,
I know just how they felt.

Her one little kindness saved my life,
though I never told her how bad things had been,
She didn't know that I had planned to end it all,
she was simply looking for a friend.

"To every thing there is a season, and a time to every purpose under the heaven: A time to be born, and a time to die; a time to plant, and a time to pluck up that which is planted; A time to kill, and a time to heal; a time to break down, and a time to build up; A time to weep, and a time to laugh; a time to mourn, and a time to dance;"

Ecclesiastes 3:1-4

Life … Under Construction

I started on my journey of life,
The road it seemed so smooth,
I had no obstacles in my way,
It was easy to make my move.

My destination was all mapped out,
I knew which way to go,
I thought I'd have sunshine all the way,
Then it started to snow.

The seasons changed my plans,
I hit some bumps on that road of mine,
The surface was cracking and potholes appeared,
It was under construction all the time.

Detour signs seemed to pop up,
At the most inconvenient place,
I had to switch gears and set a new course,
It was slowing down my pace.

It's very frustrating when you have in mind,
Just what you want to do,
But during all my struggles I've realized,
There's only One who will see me through.

God is a master worker, the Head Engineer,
He knows which path is right,
When the road seems too rugged ask for His help,
He'll guide you through the detours of life.

"And an highway shall be there, and a way, and it shall be
called The way of holiness;"

Isaiah 35:8

My MG Isn't A Sports Car

My engine was running rough, it went chug — chug all the time,
The get up and go, wasn't any more.
It was hard to tell the technician what was wrong,
I thought he would walk out the door.

My windshield was blurry and I was seeing things,
That I knew just were not there.
I needed it checked out, but it was hard to find,
Someone who would listen and care.

My poor little body was getting pretty weak,
I thought it was on its last legs.
Then the technician said "You have MG!"
And I said "Excuse me, what did you say?"

"The MG is a sports car and I know for sure,"
"One of them I own not."
He said "MG stands for Myasthenia Gravis,"
"It gets worse when the weather is hot."

I asked "A My-a-stheen-a What is?
And he said "Let me explain,"
"It's a disease that affects the neurotransmitters,"
"And to diagnose it can really be a pain."

"Your eyes will see double, your energy will be low,"
"And you'll feel like you're losing your mind,"
"But once we find out and we give you some medication,"
"You'll feel better at least some of the time."

Not many have it so it's hard to diagnose,
Some doctors still don't know what to do.
Many will have trouble eating or walking,
And sometimes it'll feel like the flu.

People will say "Hey you look great!"
Even though you feel awful inside,
They don't know what it takes to simply get dressed,
Or have the energy to go for a ride.

But if God gave you this, He knows you are tough,
And He'll be there to help you get through.
So keep your spirits up and rest when you must,
And always keep your chassis cool!

(For more information on Myasthenia Gravis,
please see the last page of this book.)

"Wherefore lift up the hands which hang down, and the feeble knees; And make straight paths for your feet, lest that which is lame be turned out of the way; but let it rather be healed. Follow peace with all men, and holiness, without which no man shall see the Lord:"

Hebrews 12:12-14

Boy — Do I Need A Tune-Up!

I walked into the office, and much to my dismay,
I saw all these body parts, arms and eyes and legs.

I went up to the receptionist, "I have an appointment," I said.
She said "Tune-ups? Down the hall, this is for parts that are dead."

The expression on my face, I can vividly recall,
Was that of a blank stare, as I walked on down the hall.

When I reached my destination, I walked in and took a seat,
An assistant came by with a bag, it contained a pair of feet.

When my name was called I stood up and paused a moment there,
I hesitated to go in, but my system was in need of repair.

When the technician came in I looked up, and nearly hit the floor,
For it wasn't whom I was expecting, but Jesus walking through that door.

He took a seat in front of me, and asked just why I came?
I told Him I knew that something was wrong, that I didn't feel the same.

He said "Well, let's take a look, and I'll tell you if there's a kink."
His manner was so kind, that it really made me think.

After looking me all over He said, "I can tell you what's gone wrong,"
"You've been working really hard, and pushing yourself much too long."

"I need to slow you down a bit, and bring you to your knees."
"You've taken me out of your life, and are doing just as you please."

"I'll let you choose, my friend, for I gave you all free will."
"Would you like to put your life in order, or suffer and pay the bill?"

I agreed to turn my life over, then asked with an inquiring face,
"What about all those body parts, that I saw out in that space?"

He said "My child I build people up, for greater things ahead."
"So when they go through tragedies or illnesses put them in bed,"

"It's not that I'm punishing people, for I love my children so dear,"
"I'm building their strength and character,
So when I call them they'll have no fear."

"And it shall be said in that day, Lo, this is our God; We have waited for him, and he will save us: this is the Lord; we have waited for him, we will be glad and rejoice in his salvation."

Isaiah 25:9

And God Said… "Your Washer Fluid Is Low!"

Driving to church one Easter morning,
My daughter was with me too,
She was searching through the radio stations,
Trying to find some good tunes.

She came across a church service,
We only had a short way to go,
The minister was preaching "And God said,"
Just then my car announced "Your washer fluid is low."

The timing couldn't have been more perfect,
And we laugh about it until this day,
God knows when we are running low,
When we are lost and have gone astray.

I always thought that I was in control,
But that message has stayed on my mind,
When things don't go the way I've planned,
I remember God knows what we need all the time.

"I WILL love thee, O Lord, my strength. The Lord is my rock, and my fortress, and my deliverer; my God, my strength, in whom I will trust; my buckler, and the horn of my salvation, and my high tower."

Psalm 18:1-2

Mr. Fix It

Screwdrivers, pliers, hammers and a wrench,
In his workshop you'll see parts all over the bench.

He's so determined, to fix all in his path,
He has tools for the car, the sink and the bath.

Our Mr. Fix Its, we love them so dear,
But when they start projects, we don't want to be near.

He'll be like an engine, full steam ahead,
Oops, he hits his hand with a hammer, his face gets all red.

Everything he starts will be so easy, he thinks,
But some projects are more complicated, like working on the sinks.

We hear the clank — clank — clank, as he works on the pipes,
Full of much perspiration, his forehead he wipes.

There is one thing that needs fixing, that he can't repair,
Though he wishes he could, and he would do it with care.

It's when his wife is sick, he doesn't know what to do,
Men want to fix everything, but he can't fix her too.

It's so hard for him to be patient, and sit idly by,
With such a helpless feeling, he'd just like to cry.

But he's a man, so his composure he'll keep,
Just prays to the Lord, as he watches her sleep.

He knows this one thing, has to be turned over to God,
So he prays as he sits there, and he begins to sob.

And when she wakes up, he kisses her so light,
Saying "God will help us get through, it will be all right."

With God by their side, and love in their hearts,
No obstacle before them, will tear them apart.

Their promise to each other, a promise for life,
Will make their love stronger, through trials and strife.

"Beloved, let us love one another: for love is of God; and every one that loveth is born of God, and knoweth God."

I John 4:7

Love Is ...

(Men and women don't always communicate on the same level, but SHOWING how much you love someone is more important than just saying it.)

Love is ... A glance, a wink, the touch of a hand.

Love is ... A kind act, a gentle word spoken, a whisper.

Love is ... Helping in a calm manner.

Love is ... Trying to think on each other's level.

Love is ... Sharing the housework.

Love is ... A loving note placed where it can be found.

Love is ... Doing something special for each other.

Love is ... Two hearts alone for an hour.

Love is ... Calming frazzled nerves with a simple embrace.

Love is ... Quiet music and candlelight.

Love is ... Taking the time to do the little things.

Love is ... Remembering what brought you together in the first place.

Love is ... Dancing to your own music, anytime.

Love is ... Knowing that someone will be there on the worst of days.

Love is ... A tender kiss, a gentle voice.

Love is ... Sometimes just a fleeting moment or it can be Always and Forever!

"The words of a man's mouth are as deep waters, and the
wellspring of wisdom as a flowing brook."

Proverbs 18:4

How Much Do You Care?

There are people who walk around, with their noses in the air,
Telling everyone how good they are, and shouting orders everywhere.

They tell you how wonderful their life is,
and the adventures that they've had,
They act like they're the best, and they can really make you mad.

Every time you see them, they have so much to say,
The important meetings in their life, and the events of their day.

They are not loving people, because they are so bold,
They have an aura about them, that gives a chill so cold.

They try to tell everyone, just how much they know,
How much they are worth, and all the places that they go.

Then there are others, who are not at all that way,
They are fun to be around, because they ask about your day.

They are interested in your life, and what has been new,
They ask how the family is, and they cheer you when you're blue.

They carry a warmth in their hearts, and smile on their face,
Their arms are open for giving hugs, in such a wonderful way.

People like to be around them, because they are so kind,
They bring out the best in others,and find out what's on their mind.

These are the type of friends to be,
To support others and always be there,
People don't care how much you know,
They want to know how much you care!

"By the word of the Lord were the heavens made; and all the host of them; by the breath of his mouth. He fashioneth their hearts alike; he considereth all their works."

Psalm 33:6,15

The Doctors Who Work With God

Illnesses and surgeries,
Broken bones and weakened hearts,
When trying to find a good physician,
It's hard to know where to start.

Many doctors act like they are God,
Like they're better than the rest.
They don't always take time to listen,
Just quickly order tests.

But I've found a special physician,
Who really takes the time,
To listen to the patients,
And asks what's on their mind.

The day I needed surgery,
Before we got underway,
The priest was saying a blessing,
And the doctor asked if she could pray.

She told us that she starts her mornings,
By asking the Lord to be her guide,
She praises God for her talents,
And asks Him to work at her side.

She said "When I chose to be a doctor,
I had many challenges in my way,"
"I asked for God's help to give me strength,
And I still do it each day."

Now I was just amazed by this,
But it really gave me peace of mind,
That there are doctors who work with God,
And treat their patients so kind.

"And if it seem evil unto you to serve the Lord, choose you this day whom ye will serve; whether the gods which your fathers served that were on the other side of the flood, or the gods of the Am'or-ites, in whose land ye dwell: but as for me and my house, we will serve the Lord."

Joshua 24:1

God's Cell Phone

(Are we as connected as we thinketh?)

THIS IS THE DAY … this is the age,
When everyone carries a cell phone!
It's great for work or pleasure,
And handy if you get stuck in the snow.

BUT … are we as connected as we think?
I got a surprise just the other day,
My cell phone rang so I looked at the numbers,
And the first thing I thought was "NO WAY!"

It read 1-800-GOD-CELL,
I just couldn't believe my eyes,
Someone must have been playing a prank on me,
But for some reason I looked toward the sky.

My phone rang again the same number appeared,
So this time I said "HELLO?"
The voice on the other end said "Are you there?"
It sounded so strong, but yet quite low.

I said "Yes, Who is this?"
He answered "Don't you recognize my voice?"
"I've been trying to get connected with you,"
"But you are so busy, you gave me no choice!"

"I figured that this might be the way to reach you,"
"Everyone is connected these days,"
"So I decided to use My cell phone to call,"
"You don't come to see me so there was no other way."

"I know that you're getting together with friends,"
"On Sunday before all of your big plans start,"
"Gather your friends and meet me at my place first,"
"I've got great entertainment and there's plenty of places to park!"

He hung up and I still couldn't believe my ears,
I stood there with the phone in my hand,
I did as He said, called all of my friends,
And told them "I just talked with the 'HEAD' Man!"

Now my group gathers on Sunday mornings,
For an hour of worship and praise,
It's a wonderful way to start off our weeks,
And I've reconnected with God in so many ways.

The Courage To Walk Alone

There will come a point in life,
No matter what they say,
When each of us will walk alone,
And go our different ways.

It doesn't really matter,
Whether a separation or death,
Finding the courage to walk alone,
Is what God helps us with the best.

CHAPTER 7

When The Road Divides

"I WILL lift up mine eyes unto the hills, from whence cometh my help. My help comes from the Lord, which made heaven and earth. He will not suffer thy foot to be moved: he that keepeth thee will not slumber. Behold, he that keepeth Israel shall neither slumber nor sleep. The Lord is thy keeper: the Lord is thy shade upon thy right hand. The sun shall not smite thee by day, nor the moon by night. The Lord shall preserve thee from all evil: he shall preserve thy soul. The Lord shall preserve thy going out and thy coming in from this time forth, and even for evermore."

Psalm 121:1-8

A Mission Into Heaven

(In memory of the crews of the Space Shuttles
Columbia and Challenger)

They were on a mission ... a journey to the stars,
To explore above the Earth, a place that seems so far.

They were on a mission ... two separate crews with a call,
A dream many of them had, since they were small.

They were on a mission ... so brave and so proud,
Fearless to fly above the world, far beyond the clouds.

They were on a mission ... each one had a task,
The Columbia complete their work and now were heading back.

They were on a mission ... we don't know what went wrong,
Their journey took them into heaven, with God where they belong.

They were on a mission ... exploring to help mankind,
We pray for their families and friends, the ones they left behind.

They were on a mission ... HEROES forever more,
God gathered them together and walked them to His Door!

They were on a mission ... now where God awaits,
The Columbia and the Challenger flew through those pearly gates.

"The Lord is my shepherd; I shall not want. He maketh me to lie down in green pastures: he leadeth me beside the still waters. He restoreth my soul: he leadeth me in the paths of righteousness for his name's sake. Yea, though I walk through the valley of the shadow of death, I will fear no evil: for thou art with me; thy rod and thy staff they comfort me. Thou preparest a table before me in the presence of mine enemies: thou anointest my head with oil; my cup runneth over. Surely goodness and mercy shall follow me all the days of my life: and I will dwell in the house of the Lord forever."

Psalm 23:1-6

Turn Now To God, Don't Turn Away!

(Dedicated in *MEMORY* of those who were lost 9-11-01, with
THANKS to all of the workers who risked their lives, with
PRAYERS for all of our Military sons and daughters who may be
called to fight a future battle, and with *BLESSINGS* to all of
families that have been left behind.)

Why did this happen? Why this way?
So many lives gone, on this tragic day.

Will we ever find answers? Who will pay?
TURN NOW TO GOD, DON'T TURN AWAY!

He was there with those people high in the sky.
He had an army of angels all ready to fly.

He gathered the pain from everyone there,
And let them know of His love and care.

He gave them the strength and courage within,
For it's not death, but a new life with Him.

Our day stopped silent with these terrible sights,
But we are a strong nation ready to fight.

Not with an enemy, but for our strength today,
TURN NOW TO GOD, DON'T TURN AWAY!

He will give us the peace and comfort we need,
We will find that helping others is better than greed.

For the loved ones we lost it's comforting to say,
THEY TURNED THEN TO GOD, THEY DIDN'T TURN AWAY!

"The Lord is good, a strong hold in the day of trouble;
and he knoweth them that trust in him."

Nahum 1:7

The Loss Of A Love

The love we held,
A love so dear,
Now has gone away.

My emotions are torn,
I feel so frail,
Can I go on another day?

Why did this happen?
Why to me?
My heart has been ripped from inside.

I hoped it would last,
I loved you so much,
Now I want to curl up and hide.

This place so dark,
So all alone,
I spend my time and cry.

Without a purpose,
Without a love,
All I want to do is die.

Someone is knocking,
Who can it be?
I open the door with fear.

He takes my hand,
Walks me out,
He says "I'm always here!"

I see sunshine again,
It's mighty bright,
The dark clouds fade away.

My spirits are lifted,
I feel renewed,
Now I walk with the Lord each day.

"Fear thou not; for I am with thee: be not dismayed; for I am thy God: I will strengthen thee; yea, I will help thee; yea, I will uphold thee with the right hand of my righteousness."

Isaiah 41:10

"Fear Not My Child"

Fear not my child, for I am watching over you,
Turn to me for guidance, I will light your way.

Fear not my child, for I am at your side,
When doubt sets in, I'll be with you as you pray.

Fear not my child, for your strength will come back,
You've always been tough, so fight hard today.

Fear not my child, your time is not over yet,
The ones who love you most are near, enjoy every day.

Fear not my child, for the challenges in your life,
Were building your courage, for this journey today.

Fear not my child, I am always by your side,
When it's time to come home, I will show you the way.

"Jesus said unto her, I am the resurrection, and the life: he ·
that believeth in me, though he were dead, yet shall he
live: And whosoever liveth and believeth in me shall
never die."

John 11:25-26

It's Time To Go

His body so limp and worn from pain,
His breathing so raspy and hard,
The agony on the face of his wife,
As she holds his hand through the bar.

He has now reached the time of the great divide,
He's living between two different plains.
His wife says "I Love You, please don't leave."
But she knows that death will release his pain.

She bends over the rail and kisses his head,
She knows it's his time to go,
His vitals are growing weaker,
And his breathing begins to slow.

He sits up and gets out of his bed,
Kisses his wife saying "I Love You Dear."
"The Lord has come to walk me home,"
"I must go now, please have no fear."

God puts his arm around the man's shoulder,
Saying "I welcome you my friend,"
"I've come to take you to my heavenly home,"
"And to your wife the angels I'll send."

Now the man realized his pain was gone,
And he could walk among the clouds so free,
He hated to leave his wife behind,
But for now that's the way it has to be.

God says "Don't worry my friend, she'll be all right,"
"Trust me and have no fear,"
"The angels will be by her side,"
"They'll watch her with love and care."

"I sought the Lord, and he heard me, and delivered me
from all my fears."

Psalm 34:4

So Close, But Yet So Far Away

You walk into my room and I see your face,
I know who you are,
But I can't come up with your name.

I feel as if I'm being robbed somehow,
I try to hang on,
But each day I slip further away.

You talk about things from my past,
I remember some of them,
Many are stories which I don't recall.

I have so much to tell you before I am lost forever,
Like, I will always love you,
And I'm scared of what is happening to me.

I know what I want to say, but I can't get it out,
Hold me close and let me know,
That you will never forget who I am.

I can tell that seeing me this way,
Is very hard on you.
Thank you for coming to visit anyway.

The days are so different now,
I'm stuck in a shell of a body,
No way to communicate with any one.

I pray in silence to the Lord,
He knows why this is happening,
And what my purpose is.

I know that some day I will get my answers,
I will be able to talk and run free,
And I know that I will be able to hold you again.

So, for now, please be strong,
I will remember you, my dear,
When we walk together in the heavens.

"And it shall come to pass in the day that the Lord shall give thee rest from thy sorrow, and from thy fear, and from the hard bondage wherein thou wast made to serve."

Isaiah 14:3

"In Heaven's Garden"

Cry for them ... NOT!
But remember them with HAPPY thoughts!

A marriage that blossomed, winter to fall,
Many years together, they grew stronger through it all.

They held hands, to comfort their fears,
He was tough, she had many tears.

You could see love in their eyes, as they walked along,
Or as they glided across the dance floor, to the "Anniversary Song."

They watched their family grow, and oh what fun,
With children and grandchildren, their love just went on.

They delighted in having fun, with family and friends,
Though their health deteriorated, they enjoyed life 'til the end.

They're not here with us now, but we don't need to cry,
Because they're in Heaven's Garden, a beautiful place in the sky.

Filled with sunshine and birds, flowers abound,
They won't get tired anymore, like they did on the ground.

I'm sure they've found peace, no more suffering or pain,
And they'll be waiting in Heaven's Garden, until we can join them again.

"I WILL sing of the mercies of the Lord forever: with my mouth will I make known thy faithfulness to all generations."

Psalm 89:1

The Angels Of Hospice Hope

(With great APPRECIATION to all who work with Hospice
programs.)

He had dignity, she had class,
But their time on Earth, was going fast.
They didn't want to burden others, but yet they knew,
They couldn't do it alone, they needed help to get through.

A hand to hold, a hand to touch,
A caring smile, that meant so much.
A time to talk, a time to pray,
Someone to give them strength, along the way.

Those special people, who understand,
Who do what they can, to lend a hand,
The Hospice workers, we hold them dear,
Because they help others go, without any fear.

Their journey was hard, they fought so long,
They put a smile on their face, and wanted to live on.
Hospice gave them comfort, took the pain away,
So they could enjoy life, until the very last day.

That final journey, we all await,
When we need others, to help us to that gate.
The young, the old, the rich, the poor,
Will travel some day, to that heavenly door.

It's wonderful to know, it was wonderful to see,
How Hospice cares for people, with dignity.
They respected their wishes, and helped them cope,
They are the loving angels, of Hospice Hope.

"And Ruth said, Intreat me not to leave thee, or to return from following after thee: for whither thou goest, I will go; and where thou lodgest, I will lodge: thy people shall be my people, and thy God my God:"

The Book of Ruth 1:16

CHAPTER 8

The Trails Of Yesteryear

"The Lord will give strength unto his people; the Lord will bless his people with peace."

Psalm 29:11

A Stop In Time!

Sitting on the porch, on a warm summer's eve,
Taking a quiet walk, through the crispy fall leaves,
Sitting by a lake, and watching the sunset,
These are the things, we sometimes forget.

Carefree days, with picnics at the park,
Listening to children, playing games in the dark,
Flying a kite, so high in the sky,
The simple times, of days gone by.

Going to the ice cream stand, was sheer delight,
Watching the stars, on a hot summer's night,
Taking the family, for a leisurely ride,
Drive-in theaters, with screens so wide.
People greeting each other, as they walk down the street,
Taking time to talk, to the strangers they'd meet,
Kids playing marbles, jump rope and tag,
They had fresh air and sunshine, to fill up their day.

Watching the magic of fireflies, as night would fall,
Relaxing in the summer, a glass of lemonade so tall,
The whispers, in the sweethearts ears,
Children growing up, with nothing to fear.

Going fishing on the pond, so peaceful it looked like glass,
Sitting under a shade tree, in the soft summer grass,
Children climbing hills, and watching their might,
As they helped each other up, instead of having a fight.

Now the days have changed, they go by so fast,
It really does us good, to remember the past,
With all of the meetings, we have to keep in our minds,
It's refreshing to the soul, to take a STOP IN TIME!

"If the Lord delight in us, then he will bring us into this land, and give it us; a land which floweth with milk and honey."

Numbers 14:8

The Church Bells Are Calling

Growing up in a little town,
You could hear those church bells chime,
They had the most beautiful sound,
I remember them in my mind.

Ding, Dong, Ding, Dong,
We could always hear them ring,
Whether church was starting or on the hour,
Throughout the air they'd sing.

As I grew older,
My career began to change,
I moved to a great big city,
My life was rearranged.

In that big old city,
I was lost among it all,
The cars, the noise, the crowds, the light,
The buildings were so tall.

No one seemed to care as much,
As they did in that town of mine,
So when I feel all confused,
I think of how those bells would chime.

I take a drive to a little town,
I remember them so dear,
I sit and listen for the church bells,
Again my mind is cleared.

Now I feel so free,
From my worries of my day,
I'll always know when life gets tough,
I can take some time to pray!

"Be ye strong therefore, and let not your hands be weak: for your work shall be rewarded."

2 Chronicles 15:7

Homemade With Love

Her hair snow white, her soul so wise,
Her passion to give, the sparkle in her eyes.

She walked so slow, yet so content,
Her hands they trembled, her fingers bent.

If you walked into Grandma's home, soon you would know,
That you've entered the house, of a God-caring soul.

There was a wonderful scent, that filled the air,
Her homemade goodies, baked with care.

She didn't have much money, but with her time,
She made goodies for all, she was so kind.

With her caring ways, and the warmth of her love,
I knew God was guiding her, from up above.

When Christmas came around, I remember so well,
Her house would be filled, with all those wonderful smells.

As we opened our presents, one by one,
I think it was Grandma, who was having the fun.

I watched the smile on her face, the tears in her eyes,
As we'd munch into her goodies, with excited surprise.

Of any tradition, that could be passed on today,
Grandma's homemade goodies, will be ours to stay!

"There is nothing better for a man, than that he should eat and drink, and that he should make his soul enjoy good in his labour. This also I saw, that it was from the hand of God."

Ecclesiastes 2:24

Steak And Eggs For Breakfast

Steak and eggs for breakfast,
Everyone would say,
Was the way to gather the family,
And get ready for the day.

Everyone lived on farms,
Our families were big,
We all had chores to do,
We didn't have fancy rigs.

Our days began at dawn,
As the sun would start to gleam.
Feeding animals or plowing fields,
We all worked as a team.

We learned to help each other,
No one could walk away,
Until all the cows were milked,
And we finished for the day.

Sure our chores were hard,
But the lessons that grew from there,
Taught us that family really mattered,
We all had to help and share.

Remember when your life gets hectic,
And all are going their own way,
Have steak and eggs for breakfast,
And family time to start your day.

"And be renewed in the spirit of your mind;"

Ephesians 4:23

The Peppermint Angel

Warm spice from apple pies, meatloaf and fresh baked bread,
Potato salad, fried chicken and homemade cookies,
These memories I'll never forget.

Her house was always filled with wonderful scents,
But there is one scent I'll remember the most,
The smell of peppermint.

Peppermint was grandma's favorite, it always filled the air.
She had peppermint rub for her hands and feet,
And she always had candies to share.

Grandma said that peppermint would help her aches and pains,
She kept a jar filled with peppermint candy on her table,
She said they would soothe her stomach again.

As kids we could help ourselves to the candy, oh what a special treat,
I still remember as it melted in my mouth,
So calming and so sweet.

Grandma has been gone for many years, but I know she is still near,
At a low point in my life the strangest thing happened,
The scent of peppermint was here.

At first it never dawned on me, why this strange thing was going on,
But then I remembered asking God for some help,
Something to help me be strong.

I started to smell peppermint and thought I had lost my mind,
But I believe that God listens to our prayers,
He sends angels to help us through tough times.

I remembered grandma's smile and all of the nice things that she did,
I remembered her determination to enjoy life and help others,
Somehow that gave me strength to live.

Now when life starts getting me down,
I do what my Peppermint Angel use to do,
I get a bag of those sweet candies to share,
Peppermint always helps me through.

"He sendeth the springs into the valleys, which run among the hills. He watereth the hills from his chambers: the earth is satisfied with the fruit of thy works."

Psalm 104:10,13

The Little Churches In The Valley

Tucked down in the valleys,
Beneath the mountains high,
You can always find a church,
I've often wondered why?

Standing there for generations,
You can see them by the light of the stars,
They were built throughout the countryside,
People came by wagons, trains or cars.

They look so inviting,
Their steeples held up high,
Their bells would call for miles,
"Come worship beneath the sky!"

When you take a step inside,
The world will seem to stop,
It takes you back to the simple days,
When God's place was on top.

With priorities in order,
Families came, one and all,
To worship and pray together,
The faith was their strong call.

The mountains represent their struggles,
The valleys, the low points in their life,
But God was their salvation,
To get them through their strife.

Yes, the little churches in the valley,
Have great meaning for us today,
They teach us, when all feels lost,
We can still turn to God and pray!

"Thou hast made known to me that ways of life; thou shalt make me full of joy with thy countenance."

Acts 2:28

Grandma's Big Old Rocking Chair

When I was a little girl,
I would climb on Grandma's lap,
In her big old rocking chair,
To cuddle for a nap.

When I got a little older,
In that big old rocking chair,
Grandma told me many stories,
While she softly brushed my hair.

As a frightened teenage girl,
When the world didn't seem fair,
I would sit and talk to Grandma,
While she rocked in her big chair.

On my Wedding Day,
The greatest gift received,
Was that big old rocking chair,
That Grandma gave to me.

Now that I have children,
We rock in that big old chair,
With all its creaking sounds,
I remembered how Grandma cared.

Though she's no longer with us,
I know her love is there,
Every time I sit and rock,
In Grandma's Big Old Rocking Chair.

"I have fought a good fight, I have finished my course, I have kept the faith:"

II Timothy 4:7

A Walk With Faith

Faith walked with us for many years,
In many different ways,
A wife, a mother, a sister, an aunt,
For our beloved Faith we pray.

Faith walked with us down life's road,
Filled with good times and with bad,
Faith walked us through the trials,
Some happy and some sad.

Faith is now in the gardens,
Of the heavens up on high,
Held in the hands of God,
Faith will be our guide.

Lord we ask you to walk with us,
And give us all your strength,
Until the time when we again,
Can walk alone with Faith.

"If I take the wings of the morning, and dwell in the uttermost parts of the sea; Even there shall thy hand lead me, and thy right hand shall hold me."

Psalm 139:9

The Pioneers

The pioneers, an adventurous group of people,
Traveling across this country in wagons,
They were a determined breed.

The pioneers, no maps to guide them,
Large families, cattle and all,
Looking for ways to succeed.

The pioneers, no roads to follow,
Only trails filled with sticks and stones,
They had a perseverance to find a way.

The pioneers, let nothing stop them,
Not rain storms, sleet or snow,
The real heroes of yesterday.

The pioneers stuck together,
Through the good times and bad,
Living off the land.

The pioneers were "Never Quit" people,
Paving the way for the future,
They really took a stand.

The pioneers, dreamers and believers,
They taught us many lessons,
About forging their way through.

The pioneers encouraged each other,
Turned to God in times of trouble,
And thanked Him in the good times, too.

There are pioneers among us now,
Who make or create a way, they inspire others to venture on,
And they still take God as their partner today.

"Lord, thou hast been our dwelling place in all generations. Before the mountains were brought forth, or ever thou hadst formed the earth and the world, even from everlasting to everlasting, thou art God."

Psalm 90:1-2

The "Greens" Are In The Freezer

The "Greens" are in the freezer,
Grandma would always say,
Since the great depression,
She didn't trust the banks.

She kept her money in containers,
Neatly tucked away,
Underneath all her baked goods,
For those "Rainy days."

Though her learn'n wasn't great,
Grandma was very smart,
She said "The greatest treasures can't be bought,"
"Only carried in your heart."

She didn't have a lot to offer,
But I've always known,
That the greatest place in the world,
Was right inside her home.

Everyone was welcome there,
She had the greatest smile,
Young and old alike,
Would visit for a while.

She could make your heart dance,
With the sparkle in her eye,
Yet lend a caring shoulder,
For those that needed to cry.

The lessons that I've learned from her,
I'm really glad to say,
Aren't stored like the "Greens" in the freezer,
But are in my heart to stay!

"For what is a man advantaged, if he gain the whole world, and lose himself, or be cast away?"

Luke 9:25

The Richest Man

He had not a cent to his name, yet his wealth went far and wide,
It was not the clothes he wore, but what he carried inside.

He had a simple little manner, and in his simple little way,
He went around spreading cheer to others, to brighten up their day.

A title - he had not one, but everyone knew his name,
They had no idea where he was from,
But they always knew when he came.

For in his path people were grinning, sometimes from ear to ear,
He had a passion for living life, and he taught people to have no fear.

The children would gather around, and sit to listen to his stories,
He always gave praise to God, and told of all His glory.

He walked everywhere he went, and people would sometimes stare,
At times he'd be toting a wounded animal, to show how much he cared.

His house was a tiny place, but with love it was always overfilled,
People went to get his advice, and his wisdom could give you a chill.

It was in those times that he'd reach out, for that man had so much love,
He knew what it was like to have crosses to bear,
And asked guidance from the One above.

He had not a cent to his name, yet his message will go on through time,
He was not remembered for his wealth, but for the riches he carry inside.

"The Lord is my strength and song, and he is become my salvation: he is my God, and I will prepare him an habitation; my father's God, and I will exalt him."

Exodus 15:2

While The Music Is In My Soul

Everyone would gather around the piano, and listen to the tunes,
Some would sing and harmonize, others could really croon.

Our lives were very simple then, that's all we had to do,
We didn't have TVs or computers, we had music to get us through.

The young and old would all join in, each would take their turn,
To show the others how they could play,
Or a new song that they had learned.

Practices were nightly, but on the weekends we would really have a ball,
Family, friends and neighbors, would gather one and all.

We would sing all the gospel hymns, or the tunes that came from war,
Everyone would relax, after they were finished with the chores.

Some would sing, some would dance, others just sat and watched,
Now with life so busy, I long for those times when I feel lost.

The older folks would say, "Never let the music in your soul end,"
"Always have a dream in your heart,
And keep the Lord close as your friend."

I would listen as they talked for hours, they always seemed so wise,
They were the kindest people, who had dreams that reached the sky.

To this day I remember their advice, though life has taken its toll,
I'll never give up, I'll always go on, while the music is still in my soul.

"Behold, the Lord thy God hath set the land before thee:
go up and posses it, as the Lord God of thy fathers hath
said unto thee; fear not, neither be discouraged."

Deuteronomy 1:21

CHAPTER 9

Enjoy The Journey

"Enter into his gates with thanksgiving, and into his courts with praise: be thankful unto him, and bless his name. For the Lord is good; his mercy is everlasting; and his truth endureth to all generations."

Psalm 100:4-5

Who Is In Your Garden?

Welcome to my garden, where the blossoms grow so tall.
A place of peace and tranquility, where I come when I hear God's call.

Here I have planted daisies,
for friends and family who have helped me out.
Over there are the violets,
for the people who took me about.

I have many sunflowers, for those who have brightened my days,
And several rows of tulips, for the strangers that God sent my way.

In the outer corners of my garden, the lilies reach toward the sky,
For the special people who gave me comfort, when I needed to cry.

The morning glories are planted,
for the people I've helped along the way.
The gardenias are near the bench,
to remind me of those in trouble when I pray.

Bleeding hearts are in the middle, one for each person who is gone.
Roses are by the cross of the Lord, to give me the strength to go on.

I love to look at my garden, whenever it starts to rain,
There's always a beautiful rainbow,
to remind me that God's in control again.

And once the rains are over, my garden has a golden glow,
The rainbow ends in the center, for those people are my true pots of gold.

"But as truly as I live, all the earth shall be filled with the glory of the Lord."

Numbers 14:21

A Simple "Thank You"

"GOD, give me this!" And "GOD, I want that!"
What's the Lord to do?
With all the requests we place on Him,
It could really make Him blue.

Demands and questions and prayers for help,
Could wear our poor God out!
Wars and fighting and people depressed,
Asking "What's life all about?"

We put so much pressure on the One above,
More and more each day,
Did you ever think He might get tired,
Or need a simple "Thank You" today.

We always know He's going to be there,
To lighten up our load,
But where are we when He needs us most,
To take His message down the road?

Think of what will happen when you reach heaven,
And He looks up your name,
How many times will it be listed there,
For all the thanks you gave?

Will you slump over and say "Sorry Lord,"
"I gave less than I took!"
Or will you stand up proud, because you gave more,
When He looks in His Golden Book?

Remember there's a saying that simply goes,
You'll get back ten-fold that which you give,
You better start saying "Thanks God" today,
For you never know how much longer you'll live!

"This is the day which the Lord hath made; we will rejoice and be glad in it."

Psalm 118:24

Enjoy Today

I wake up in the morning, and my decision is already made,
No matter what the weather is like, I must enjoy this day!

I may have aches and pains, that make it hard to get out of bed,
But if I don't enjoy today, tomorrow I could be dead.

People often go on complaining, about what they'd like their life to be,
Always rushing into tomorrow, trying to find things to set them free.

But I've learned through many struggles, searching high and low,
That happiness can't be bought, it comes from in your soul.

There is something that's inside of us, tucked deep within the heart,
A special thing called happiness, it's renewed as each day starts.

It's your choice of how you use it, but wasting it will make you sad,
Happiness can brighten your day, you'll enjoy the time you had.

There may be bumps in your road of life, each of us has them these days,
Facing life with a happy heart, will help your journey all the way.

"That I may come unto you with joy by the will of God, and may with you be refreshed. Now the God of peace be with you all. Amen."

Romans 15:32-33

The Treasure Of The Tub

"Coming with us?" Someone asked,
"The day has been really rough!"
"No thanks," I politely say,
"I'm going home to my tub."

I laugh a little to myself,
For the look upon their face,
As they leave to hit the bars,
I go home to my sacred place.

I light a bunch of candles,
Soothing music fills the air,
And once I'm beneath the bubbles,
I haven't got a care.

Aromatherapy is a warming touch,
To calm a trying day,
The tub is filled with delightful scents,
And I slowly slip away.

I can't travel to far off lands,
For my weak muscles won't carry me,
But with music from around the world,
My imagination is set free.

I can be in the Hawaiian Islands,
Imagine the beautiful scenes,

Or jig among the Irish,
Where the hills are always green.

I listen to music by Beethoven,
Or that done by Bach,
I don't worry how much time I spend.
I forget about the clock.

Once I'm all refreshed,
And my troubles have floated away,
I thank God for the treasure of my tub,
To brighten up my day.

"For unto us a child is born, unto us a son is given: and the government shall be upon his shoulder: and his name shall be called Wonderful, Counsellor, The mighty God, The everlasting Father, The Prince of Peace."

Isaiah 9:6

The Christmas Gift

Christmas is a special time, of memories held so dear,
A time to send our greetings, to folks both far and near.

A time when spreading joy, should fill up all our hearts,
But sometimes this hectic season, can tear us all apart.

We forget what it's all about, and what it really means,
It's for spreading love and peace to all, not just of material things.

For on this day Jesus was born, in a stable oh so small,
He had nothing but love to give, and He gave his life for all.

Though He wasn't very old, His message went far beyond His years,
He was sent to be our Savior,
And tell us God will guide us through our fears.

Sometimes in celebrating this season,
We get depressed about it all,
Worrying about buying presents, or the crowds at the mall.

We all have the most precious gift, it's right within our hearts,
The gift called love that God gave us, is the best gift from the start.

Now it's your turn to use your gift, give a hug or lend a helping hand,
For Jesus taught us that love is THE CHRISTMAS GIFT,
So give it away whenever you can.

"Delight thyself also in the Lord; and he shall give thee the desires of thine heart. Commit thy way unto the Lord; trust also in him; and he shall bring it to pass."

Psalm 37:4-5

Thanks For Traveling With Me!

I hope you've enjoyed our journey together,
Through mountain's high and valley's low,
When faced with detours, stay off the sidewalks,
And ask God's guidance wherever you go.

We all have hopes and dreams,
God gave us those from the start,
As you shoot for the moon and reach for the stars,
Remember to carry *LOVE* within your heart.

Our journey is not over,
Until we reach those Heavenly Gates,
So no matter how rough the roads may be,
"NEVER QUIT" for goodness sake.

Wear a smile and be kind to others,
No matter how you feel,
When the road twists or turns and
you don't know where your going,
Always ask God to take the wheel!

About Myasthenia Gravis

Throughout this book I have mentioned Myasthenia Gravis and you've probably thought "What is it?" I asked that same question when my neurologist told me that I had MG. Myasthenia Gravis (MG) is a chronic autoimmune-neuromuscular disorder, which is characterized by fluctuating weakness of the voluntary muscle groups. Muscles that control movement of the arms, legs, head, neck, talking, chewing, swallowing, coughing, facial expressions and breathing may become affected. Ocular Myasthenia Gravis occurs when the muscles that control the eyes and eyelids are primarily affected.

Individuals with MG have physical symptoms that tend to fluctuate throughout the day. The symptoms from one MG patient to another also tend to vary. It is common for the fatigue to worsen as the day progresses. Rest often brings some relief. MG can be a very humbling disorder. Patients are often dependent on others for assistance. They may start their day nearly normal and be struggling with many challenges by the end. Symptoms may fluctuate from day to day and hour to hour. Activities and environmental changes can greatly affect it. Breathing problems can become a serious, potentially life-threatening complication of MG.

Because MG affects each person so differently, it is sometimes referred to as a "Snowflake" disease, no two are the same. There is no cure for MG, but there are effective treatments that allow many, but not all people with MG, to lead full lives. Common treatments include medications, thymectomy and plasmapheresis. For more information on Myasthenia Gravis, you may contact:

Myasthenia Gravis Foundation of America, Inc.
5841 Cedar Lake Rd., Suite 204
Minneapolis, MN 55416
1-800-541-5454
(www.myasthenia.org)

Printed in the United States
1226700006BA/73-534